The Stowaway Kid

The Story of Chef Alfredo

by

William Bishop

with Orthnell Alfredo Russell

DORRANCE
PUBLISHING CO
EST. 1920
PITTSBURGH, PENNSYLVANIA 15238

Dorrance Publishing Co
585 Alpha Drive
Pittsburgh, PA 15238
Visit our website at *www.dorrancebookstore.com*

ISBN: 978-1-6366-1329-1
eISBN: 978-1-6366-1909-5

INTRODUCTION

In the course of human history there are life stories and experiences that rise to the point of being worthy of books or movies, for masses of people to be made aware of, and for successive generations to learn about. The story of a Bahamian immigrant to the United States named Orthnell Alfredo Russell (Chef Alfredo) is one such story. Chef Alfredo as he became known after finding his way to Pittsburgh, PA, immigrated to the United States from the Bahamas in the 1950s, but his story of immigration is no normal story and the life that he lived in the Bahamas before emigrating and after arriving in the U.S. is anything but commonplace. Chef Alfredo as his name suggests is a culinary expert, and the story of how he became such in a land that was not his own in a time when people of African descent were not finding America the most accommodating place and White Americans not the most accepting people, sheds light on the persistence, resilience, and hope of the human spirit. This tale is inspiring and wrought with lessons from the "old school" in the city of Mastic Point on the island of Andros which is the largest island in the Bahamas, where just about everyone was Black and there were none of the comforts and conveniences enjoyed by many in the U.S. Life was difficult there, but there was a strong community, and the people of Mastic Point had a sense of pride, purpose, and belonging.

Chef Alfredo's tale of immigration begins in 1954 when he was only 15 years old and stowed away on a cruise ship that was headed to Florida with nothing but an idyllic dream of making a better life for himself in America.

He had no change of clothes and only a few dollars when he stowed away, but this is where his faith in God, ingenuity, and determination came in. Although he had been to the U.S. before with his uncle as a contract farm laborer his act of stowing away was a more serious, permanent decision. For many people reading this, it would seem far-fetched for a teenager to make such a serious decision, but once you learn about the society that Chef grew up in and the expectations placed on young men from the age of 12 (the age where boys were expected to accept the responsibilities of manhood) it all becomes more believable.

His journey took him from the Bahamas, to Miami, Florida, then to New York City and Peekskill, New York, back home to the Bahamas briefly and then to Jacksonville, Florida, and finally to Pittsburgh, Pennsylvania. It was wrought with brushes with immigration authorities, and people and places who did not always understand him and vice versa. He had jobs that ranged from farm laborer to dish washer, butler and chauffer to short order cook, musician and band leader to executive chef and restaurateur. Before leaving the Bahamas for good, Chef lived a challenging life, spent time at a Catholic monastery, knew more work than play as a boy, and eventually became a self-made man, husband, father, and entrepreneur in America.

His permanent life in the U.S. would not begin until he was about 20 years old. He remained in the U.S. after stowing away at 15 for over 3 years before returning home. He then was hired by a wealthy White couple from Jacksonville, FL whom he met while operating a tour boat in the Bahamas to be their chauffeur and butler. Chef went and worked for this family for over 3 years. It was there in Florida that he became a citizen, married, started a family, and eventually established a life for himself. He consistently found work in restaurants and solidified his future life as a chef and restaurateur. He also managed several bands and nightclubs, things that he would continue when he arrived in Pittsburgh in the early 1970s.

Chef's life and the story that is told here do not simply focus on successes and triumphs of an immigrant in America. There were also shortcomings, as with any life story. His relationships with women is one of those. Chef was born and raised in a home without a father. In fact, he didn't meet his father until he was 13. His siblings, none of whom shared a father with him, also did not grow up living with their fathers. Though it was not his intention, he continued this legacy. His first marriage in 1962 produced 2 children that he loved dearly, but it ended in divorce. The strains of being on the road with his bands, managing nightclubs, and the admiring women that accompanied this life proved too much for his young wife to bear. He would have four more children with three other women. When he left for Pittsburgh in the 70s, he left behind four children and no doubt some sadness and regret on their part. As talented and charismatic as he was and is, he was not available as a constant, day-to-day presence in his children's lives for significant parts of their upbringing. Though several of his children have been quite successful, there is no way to deny that the goal when he and his first wife wed and what they both believed was ideal was a home with children and two parents living together. But, this was not to be. Chef did marry again. This time to a woman he met in Pittsburgh, but they had no children together, and she died of cancer in 1991.

Though he didn't defy the statistics for family dynamics for people of African descent in America, he has defied other statistics not only related to African Americans, but all Americans. Only about 14% of Americans own a business and an even smaller percentage actually employ others (Buchanan). Chef has done both. Whatever Chef learned in his home country, what he saw, and experienced led him to do what not even 15 percent of Americans are able or willing to do. His mindset and approach to life have always been one of self-reliance, not dependence, and this is reflected in the three restaurants that he has owned or been a part owner of and the bands that he personally managed and performed in. He has epitomized the American way of entrepreneurship and independence.

In many ways Chef's life and experiences highlight both the struggles and triumphs of an immigrant, but also speak to things that are characteristic of the African American experience. Wherever he went in Florida, New York, or Pittsburgh, he identified with and was accepted into the Black communities there. His time in New York City is very telling about what life was like for young Blacks in Harlem and upstate New York. He fully embraced the social life and world of work in New York as he had done in Miami and would later do in Pittsburgh. One thing that shines through the pages of this book is his commitment to young men like himself. Chef rarely did anything without the thought of bringing someone along to learn and prosper with him. When he set out on his own after working for years for a wealthy White family in Florida, he took along several other young Black men so that they could find employment and stable lives as well. In Pittsburgh, in the restaurants he owned he employed and taught other Blacks the culinary arts and shared his business skills with them.

In today's world of charged dialogue concerning immigration and immigrants, Chef Alfredo's story highlights what many miss in the discourse, and that is that there have always been people in America that have wanted immigrants here. For centuries employers have sought out the immigrant for his skills, work ethic, and ingenuity. Chef is no different. As a contract laborer, a butler and chauffer, a manager of bands and nightclubs, and as a chef, he has been sought after by Americans. Almost all of those were White. There is something that immigrants like him have offered to this great country that cannot be denied. Some today, as in the past, have sought to demonize and use immigrants as scapegoats for a myriad of problems, but this is very hypocritical and untruthful. The truth is that America is as great as it is because of immigrants like Chef Alfredo and will continue to thrive and excel beyond what we can imagine in so much as we embrace the diversity and vastness of the populations that want to experience the dream that we hold so dear.

Chef Alfredo's story holds inspiration for people of many walks of life, but one that he could have never anticipated were those in the handicapped community. In May of 2009, he was in a life altering, almost fatal car crash that ultimately led to him having one of his legs amputated below the knee. At 70, the thought of going through multiple major surgeries, being hospitalized for over a year, losing a limb, and having to learn how to walk with a prosthetic leg would have caused many to want to simply end life and give up. Not Chef; he endured all of this and eventually returned to work at Bistro to Go, the restaurant that he helped start on Pittsburgh's North Side. He is truly amazing and this facet of his life contains much that will inspire anyone who is struggling back from a similar situation or facing any life challenge for that matter.

His story contains much that educates regarding the medical and rehab communities, social services, and simply navigating life as a person with a handicap after 70 years of navigating life without one. Along with work and basically every other function, he eventually also returned to driving. No longer dependent on senior or disabled van service, Chef earned a driver's license for modified vehicles and purchased a van with the gas and brake controls mounted on the steering wheel. Many would have given up, but his life to this point had taught him that great and amazing things will happen if you believe in yourself and never give up. And, that is exactly what he did.

He took the skills he had, the passion God had given him, and faith in that very same God and himself and made the life that he envisioned, conquering seemingly insurmountable feats to live the American Dream. There is triumph in his story, but there is also tragedy, but at the age of 82, he is still taking on challenges and his life provides astounding inspiration that people of all ages and all walks need. In the pages that follow, you will be educated, inspired, entertained, and uplifted. Enjoy!

UPBRINGING

Orthnell Alfredo Russell was born on June 7, 1939 to Rose Elizabeth Edden and Joshua Samuel Russell in Mastic Point on the island of Andros in the Bahamas. Even though Rose and Joshua were not, nor ever did marry, and young Orthnell did not meet his father until he was 13 years old, he was given the surname Russell and bears that name proudly to this day. In fact, Rose Edden never married any of the men who were the fathers of her 8 children. As Chef says, "she was a bachelorette until she died." Despite the fact that Rose bore the sole responsibility of raising her children, Mastic Point was a close-knit community, and there was help for her and her children from other people, namely relatives, especially Elma Edden, Rose's mother.

Orthnell was the only child born to Rose and Joshua, but as stated above, he had several siblings. His older brother Cornelius Henderson was born 4 years before him in 1935. Cornelius's father was Bruce Pickstock, the lone police officer in Mastic Point. Orthnell and "Henderson" were very close growing up and were Rose's only children until their brother Albert was born three years after Orthnell in 1942. Albert's father was Henry Munnings who also fathered 2 of Rose's other Children, William and Frank. Rose's other three children Ruth, David, and Etta Mae were fathered by Manny Lightburn.

With Rose never marrying or establishing a household with any of the men that she had children with, one is left to wonder were Joshua, Bruce,

Joseph, Henry, or Manny not up to the marriage standard for Rose or was it simply Rose's preference to remain single and raise her children as a single mother with the help of those in her community and family? When asked, Chef holds that it was never his place to ask his mother about such a personal topic. This highlights a consistent theme throughout Chef's experiences in Mastic Point and what shaped his upbringing and his worldview, and that is respect for elders and knowing one's place.

Whether speaking of family members or other members of the community Chef stresses that children "knew their place." This meant that in day-to-day interactions older members of the community and family were spoken to with respect and regarded with deference. The old adage "children speak when spoken to" definitely was applied in Mastic Point. Chef recalls referring to his elders as Sir and Ma'am, Mr. such and such and Mrs. so and so. Often in the process of writing this book Chef would speak of people only by their last name and when I would ask him the person's first name he did not know because an elders' first name was not relevant information for a child, unless that child had some reason to know the person's first name, perhaps because of a close relationship or personal dealing. There were some in the community that were referred to as Aunt or Uncle and then the person's first name would follow. This was the case even for older individuals who were not actually blood relatives. The same phenomenon existed and in some cases still does in African-American communities, where people who were close to a family or endeared to the community are affectionately referred to as Aunt or Uncle.

His days as a youngster were not filled with play as children's days are filled today. In fact he cannot recall ever having a toy as a child, and hardly remembers any games that he played. Surely, there must have been games or ways that children in Mastic Point interacted that kept them entertained, but Chef recalls more readily the chores and work that he and his siblings had to perform to help out his mother and grandmother. Not having any modern conveniences like electricity, running water, indoor plumbing, grocery stores and automobiles required great effort on everyone's part to meet the family's needs on a daily basis.

One chore that was extremely important was retrieving water. In the cluster of houses where Orthnell lived, which included about 6 families: the Carters, the Johnsons, the Rolles, the Cantors, the Taylors, and the Eddens, Orthnell's family, there was a well. In fact the well was central to the cluster,

2

but the water was brackish and only meant for washing clothes and bathing as it had too much salt content for drinking. The water that was used for drinking and cooking had to be retrieved from a spring which was about a 3 mile walk away from their home. In order to retrieve the water, Orthnell and Henderson, like everyone living in the area would walk carrying tin buckets to the spring and return with buckets full of water every couple of days. The skill in this, especially for youngsters, was to make the journey back from the spring without losing too much of the water over the sides of the buckets. Now, making a trek like this for many would be challenging enough, but adding to the difficulty was the practice of carrying the buckets on their heads. So, not only were Orthnell and Henderson carrying tin buckets of water for several miles, but one of those buckets was placed on each boy's head, being held with one hand. At the time they thought little of this. It was just customary, but he learned to carry the tin bucket on his head and lose very little water on the way, something that Rose and Elma greatly appreciated.

Along with retrieving fresh water for the family's use, there was a constant need for wood. Cooking, bathing, and washing clothes were all done outside. Immediately behind Orthnell's home was the kitchen and outhouse. The kitchen, which was an open-air structure with a pit for building a daily fire, was used of course for cooking, but also for washing clothes, as the fire served not only for preparing meals, but also for heating water for the washing and bathing. The home was used only for sleeping and protection from the elements. Wood was plentiful. Andros was not very developed and lush forests or "cuppets" as they were called, abounded. In fact, all of what the inhabitants needed for survival was available; it just required work to access it. Things like trekking miles to retrieve fresh water, or going into the cuppet to gather bundles of wood were as routine for children in Mastic Point as sitting down to play video games or watching TV for children today. So, Orthnell and Henderson, and eventually all of Orthnell's other siblings, including the girls gathered wood from the cuppet.

The vast expanses of cuppet provided another activity for Orthnell: hunting. He recalls going into the woods many times with nothing more than stones to hunt wild birds. He did this alone because Henderson did not care for hunting and the other outdoor activities that Orthnell grew to thoroughly enjoy. On the island there were wild chickens and pigeons that provided decent nutrition for the Edden family. The challenge, of course, would be killing the birds in order to bring them home. Now, Orthnell did not have a gun. In fact, no one in the Edden household did. Instead, he used stones that he would hurl with precision at unsuspecting birds. It required the use of "just the right stone." This would have been a stone that was not too large, but heavy enough to gather enough velocity to kill the bird. Needless to say, it took some skill to quietly approach a wild bird, keep far enough away so as not to scare the bird off, and propel the stone at the target before the bird was able to escape. This also may explain why Orthnell did this alone; it's easier to manage the movements and sounds made by one than two or three. Perhaps Henderson just didn't have the patience or maybe he didn't think that the reward (fresh chicken or pigeon meat) was worth the effort.

There was one instance when Orthnell, against the wishes of his mother, went hunting with two young men who did have a gun, a shotgun. The two boys were named Ivory (17) and Willie (14). Orthnell, like Willie, was close to 14 at the time. Ivory and Willie were two of the only White youngsters living in Mastic Point, and two of the very few Whites that Orthnell encountered in his childhood. They were in Mastic Point with their parents as their father owned the local sawmill, an important source of jobs for the local men and boys like Orthnell, something that will be discussed later. It is unclear why Rose urged him not to go hunting this particular time. It could have been that she had knowledge that Ivory and Willie had a gun. Or, perhaps, she had a general mistrust of Whites. Terms like Conky Joe were and still are used to refer to them, often in a pejorative sense. Or, perhaps it was simply a mothers' intuition. Whatever the reason, she urged him not to go, but he did so anyhow.

While out hunting, Ivory spotted a snipe running along the beach, raised the shotgun, and fired, sending hundreds of tiny lead bird shot in the direction of the snipe. The snipe immediately ceased moving. It was a successful kill, but something quickly put a damper on their success. In a matter of seconds, four boys came running and screaming out of a makeshift bungalow that they had built along the seashore, all of them bleeding from wounds in their lower legs as a result of the bird shot from Ivory's gun.

It turns out that three of the boys were cousins of Orthnell's and a fourth was a close friend of his family. The cousins: Nicey, Edgar, and Cubie were his Aunt Amie's children. Amie was Rose's sister-in-law. The fourth boy, Terry, was the son of Ada, a close family friend.

The boys ran and notified some adults of what happened. Someone also retrieved Bruce Pickstock, the police officer, and brought him to the scene. There were no hospitals in Andros so a plane had to be sent from Nassau if the injured boys were to receive treatment for their wounds, which is what happened. This communication took place by telegraph. It took the plane one and a half hours to finally arrive and take the boys to Princess Margaret Hospital in Nassau. It is a good thing that the boys' wounds were not in vital parts of their bodies as they may have died otherwise. The boys remained at the hospital for about 3 days and then returned home. Ivory, the one who fired the shot was questioned by officer Pickstock and let go when it became clear that he had no malicious intent.

Now, when all of the questioning and aftermath transpired Orthnell was nowhere to be found. Once he realized that his cousins and friend had been shot he immediately ran home to make sure that he appeared in front of his mother before the news of what happened reached her. After all, she had told him not to go and he went against her wishes. In the end, Orthnell and everyone involved may have been better off heeding Rose's warnings. But, no one will ever know. One thing is for sure: Orthnell never went hunting again when a gun was involved. He went back to hunting birds with stones.

It is interesting to note the freedom that these boys had. Although they were never more than a short walk from caring adults they still were permitted to venture out on their own, collaborate, and do something like hunt for wild birds with a gun. Perhaps, the shooting incident illustrates that they had too much freedom, but it also explains how a sense of independence and responsibility could have taken root in someone like Orthnell, but it wouldn't be long before this sense of independence and responsibility would lead him to set his mind on going to America.

Orthnell's response to the situation, i.e. running home and addressing Rose before the news reached her illustrates something else about Orthnell. It shows that from an early age he had a tendency to do what was necessary to protect himself. It is curious that a boy so young, who came from a tight-knit community and supportive family would up and leave those people and when asked, never indicates, at least to his biographer, that he had any qualms about that fact at all. Most questions about emotions and sentimental responses to seemingly tough decision like leaving his mother, siblings, and friends for long periods of time are met with a response similar to this: "I did what I had to do." At the forefront of his mind, even as a young teenager was the necessary steps to achieving his future goals, regardless of who may have disapproved or been hurt or disappointed by his choices. This is not mentioned to suggest a negative character flaw; it is a part of what enabled Orthnell to do the remarkable things that he did over the course of his life. Of all his siblings and most of his friends from Mastic Point, he is the only one who permanently left and charted a completely foreign path.

Not only did Orthnell hunt wild birds, he also took to the beaches for crabs of 2 varieties: blue and white. These were seasonal creatures and he had to know when the time was right for each type. But, it was a very good day when he could go to the shore and come home with a basket full of crabs for his family to eat. At times he had enough to also sell to his neighbors. Again, he did most of this alone or with local friends or cousins, not with Henderson.

Even the things that Orthnell considered to be "fun" often still had some level of utility associated with them, and aided in survival, like hunting wild birds or crabs, or "borrowing" a small rowboat that wasn't being used for the day to go fishing. If Orthnell noticed a row boat on the shore after the time when most men would have already left out to go fishing, he would help himself to it and go fishing himself. Much more about fishing will be discussed later. Even though these things were regarded as fun activities, Orthnell's goal in part was to bring home something for Rose and Elma to put in the pot and onto the table.

One activity that was done purely for fun, but still involved some work and vigilance was capturing wild dogs. On the island there were wild dogs that lived in caves and hideouts in the cuppet. He does not recall exactly what type of dogs they were, but as a youngster he made sport of capturing one or two and bringing them home. They only remained with him for a while because the dogs that he brought home were usually puppies, and eventually reclaimed during the night, under the cover of darkness, by their mothers. The boys would scare the mothers off by hurling rocks or sticks at them, and yelling and screaming.

Something else that was enjoyed by all the residents at Mastic Point were holidays. Two of the most widely celebrated holidays were Christmas (December 25th as elsewhere) and Junkanoo on December 26th. Junkanoo marks the beginning of the anticipated excitement of the coming New Year. After the celebration on the 26th there was another New Year's celebration on January 1st, but the celebration on the 26th was the biggest. It is still celebrated today. Junkanoo resembles Mardi Gras in New Orleans and Carnival in many Latin American countries in many ways. One of the main activities of the celebration is parades where participants wear creative and colorful masks and costumes. Mostly men don elaborate masks, but women and children participate by wearing their own colorful, exciting costumes. People would come out of their homes, gather along the roads and watch the procession of people. Musicians would play traditional instruments and people would sing, all in preparation for the New Year. This was and is a festive time marked by joviality, grand displays of creativity and excitement, and specially prepared Bahamian dishes.

Observing Christmas in Mastic Point was quite unique and reflects the community oriented faith and commitment of a majestic people. The Catholic and Methodist Churches were prominent in Mastic Point and the Christian Faith was almost ubiquitous. This, along with the lack of commercialization of any type made Christmas a very solemn, reflective time, where people focused more on their loved ones in their homes and their communities, not on material acquisition or shopping. The main Christmas day event took place in the Society Hall, where everyone from the community gathered for dancing and singing of spiritual songs. There was an exchange of gifts, but everyone who had anything to give, placed them under a common tree. This is very different from the Christmas celebrations of today both in the U.S. and in the Bahamas, where people, for the most part celebrate with their individual families, in the privacy of their own homes or the home of a relative. Christmas truly was a community event, and everyone in the community celebrated together from about 7:00 PM until almost midnight.

Other holidays such as Columbus Day, Boxing Day, a traditional day of shopping in the UK, and like Junkanoo, is observed on December 26th, and now Independence Day (July 10) are observed. Independence for the Bahamas came on Jul 10, 1973, years after Orthnell had already left the islands. These celebrations provided the people of Mastic Point with healthy, collective fun, and engagement in a place and time where personal, private entertainment through televisions, smart phones, and other technology did not exist. After all, holidays everywhere were created to break up the monotony of everyday life, to provide relief from the strain of work, which there was a lot of in Orthnell's world.

A BLACK WORLD

The world that Orthnell was born into was one that was almost exclusively Black, where everyone in his immediate surroundings was of African descent. To many that hail from African countries or places in the Caribbean or South America this may not seem significant, but juxtaposed with the world that Orthnell would go to where people of European descent dominated almost all spheres, it wrought a lasting and positive impact on his worldview and self-image. The European dominance that he confronted in America was not always numerical. It was manifested in the power structures and images that he saw. For instance, he lived in several predominantly Black neighborhoods, but he was well aware that the authorities and people that he had to answer to were not the people he lived around, but White police officers, immigration authorities, and employers. It was these people who controlled human interactions and Orthnell and those like him were accountable to them.

When considering the psychological effects of living in a society where images of successful people who look like one's self are somewhat scarce, and people can develop negative perceptions of themselves and their potential as a result of negative images and media as in the case of African-Americans, living in a Black world like Orthnell did while growing up, it truly had the opposite effects. As a child Orthnell witnessed a community and society that provided him with all of the essential things that a society must for human beings to thrive: education and schools, religion and churches, stores, businesses, medical care, and services through trades such as carpentry, masonry, boating, and fishing. But, unlike Africans in America, especially after full integration where many of these services were provided by and controlled by Whites, in Andros those that provided these services were all Black. In fact, Orthnell did not see a White person until he was about 12 years old. This means that he witnessed on a daily basis Black professionals of all sorts, Blacks of means, educated Blacks, Blacks who were independent, self sufficient, and highly skilled.

Naturally, two of the industries that were crucial to life in the Bahamas and most island countries were boating and fishing. Again, in a place where everyone was Black this vital industry was controlled by people of African descent. Men in Andros built boats of all types: sail boats, dinghy boats, and schooners. Many men also made their living through fishing. Men would spend weeks at a time out at sea catching a wide array of aquatic life for sale at market: several species of fish, crabs, conch, and sponge. The boats that many of the men used had live wells in them so that their catch would remain alive and fresh. The men of Andros were industrious and highly skilled providers. Orthnell too would become such a man.

One of the fishermen Orthnell knew very well was his very own uncle, Lar. Uncle Lar was Rose's sister Amie's husband and Nicey, Edgar, and Cubie's father. He was a skilled fisherman who made his living this way. Uncle Lar had his children and Amie to support and fishing provided him the income that he needed to keep his family fed and provided for. Now, Uncle Lar was not fortunate to have a large sailboat that carried a large crew and could stay out at sea for extended periods of time. This was the type of vessel that fishermen used who were able to make substantial money from their hauls that they could glean and store in the huge live wells that were built into the hull of the boat. Instead he had a rowboat that he took out to sea every day to fish and returned at night. This was a worthy occupation, but there was a clear distinction between those who owned sail boats and those who owned smaller boats like Lar's. Lar's earning potential was quite limited in comparison to those who were able to stay at sea until their live wells were full and could go further out to sea, in search of a catch, and thus anticipate their profits. Nevertheless, he worked hard and provided all of the necessities for his family.

Lar was forced to deal with the reality that in a given day he could only catch a limited amount of fish, sponge, or conch, and if it was a bad day his only recourse was the hope that tomorrow might be a better one. The downside was that he couldn't stay out at sea where he needed to fish for long periods of time. Instead he had to return home and go through the process of rowing out to sea again, something that required energy and effort, energy and effort that could be devoted to his true goal: catching valuable sea products. In this way the fishermen with sailboats had a serious advantage over those who were not fortunate to have such vessels.

One occasion illustrates how important a day's catch was to a man like Lar. When Orthnell was about 11 he had the opportunity to go out to sea with Uncle Lar. Orthnell asked his uncle if he could go with him to work; Lar agreed on the condition that he help and not hinder. Orthnell assured him that he would not get in the way and would be an asset on the boat. So, they set off one early morning together. The day proved to be productive. Orthnell and Lar caught a good number of fish.

While they were fishing things grew interesting and troubling for Orthnell as Lar saw what he believed to be the catch of the day, the largest fish they had seen yet. In the Bahamas at that time fishermen used a water glass to peer under the water and spot fish. The water glass sat on top of the water and magnified what was beneath and one could often see the fish that they then would attempt to catch. Of course only the clearest Caribbean water would allow for this type of spying. By this point the current had picked up and Lar needed Orthnell to "skull" the boat, or row it to the specific location where he needed to be. However, with him being only 11 and the water getting a bit rough, he was not able to skull the boat effectively. As he struggled, Uncle Lar became so enraged at his inability to move the boat effectively that he took a wet rope and struck him, knocking him sternly in the head. After being struck Orthnell became frightened and being a very good swimmer decided to take his chances in the sea and jumped overboard. As he began to swim he noticed that Lar was now skulling the boat in the opposite direction; indeed, instead of going to retrieve his nephew in his anger he was heading for home. Orthnell was fortunate that there was a tiny island nearby where he could rest and wait for help. And help was not long coming as another fishing boat came by and picked him up. It is not clear if Lar knew about the nearby island that would serve as a refuge for Orthnell. All Orthnell knew was that his uncle had abandoned him. Orthnell never told this story to his mother or grandmother and Uncle Lar apparently never told either because neither Rose nor Elma ever brought it up, and needless to say, Orthnell never went fishing with Uncle Lar again.

The story about Uncle Lar and Orthnell fishing highlights an interesting reality for boys in Andros, and that is that they had to grow up fast. Orthnell, at 11, and in many instances earlier than that even had to exhibit the characteristics and strength of an adult man. Lar's perspective, if not his treatment of Orthnell was shared by many adults in Andros and that was that everyone had to play their part in survival and providing for their respective families. From Uncle Lar's view there was a valuable commodity that he lost because of his nephew's lack of strength. They did not go out to sea for fun, but for survival, and if Chef was too young to aid in survival then he should have stayed home. In today's world, the thought of an 11-year-old boy being abandoned at sea by an adult would warrant charges, but not in 1950, and not in Andros.

It is interesting to think of children in the way describe above, but in a world with so little convenience, there was little time for playing and going through the various stages of childhood and adolescence that we have come to accept in modern times. Boys were expected to take on the responsibilities and characteristics of men around age 12. Perhaps for Lar, Orthnell, at 11, was close enough.

Not only was Andros filled with fishermen like Uncle Lar, but every major institution was run by Black people. As in any society, two of the most fundamental institutions were the schools and places of worship. First, let's deal with the school. I mention school in the singular because there was just one school where all children of a certain age attended, and beyond that, students had to pass a test to move on to another level in a different school. It was simply called "All Ages School" and it was located in an area referred to as The Bight. Children from ages 6 (1st Grade) to 12 or 13 (7th Grade) attended this school. They came from 4 main locations: The Bight of course, Mastic Point, Buzzard Bay, and Red Bay. It was about 2 or 3 miles from where Orthnell and his family lived, and of course as with any destination they walked there every day.

It was at this school, a one-room building that Orthnell, his siblings, and other children from Mastic Point and the other areas received their education. If students completed the program that included Mathematics, Reading, Writing, Speech, and History they graduated with a 7th grade education. Some, like Orthnell (although he only completed the 6th grade) went to work instead of going on for further education. That education could be obtained in Nassau, the Capital. There in Nassau students could obtain a high school education. Some took the required test and went on to further their education, and others did something very interesting, they became "monitors" and assisted with the education of the younger students, grades 1 through 5. In fact, Orthnell's primary education was largely facilitated by monitors as opposed to formal teachers in the sense that we think of teachers today. The two monitors that he readily recalls are Laine, a female, and Thomas, a male, both teenagers at the time.

The school was run by a schoolmaster. The schoolmaster served in the same capacity that principals do today. At the time the schoolmaster was Mr. Taylor. Mr. Taylor was a tall, dark, and very articulate man who was stern and handled well the responsibility of running the school. He was a family man with at least one daughter named Patsy. Mr. Taylor was responsible for facilitating the education for all ages and grade levels with the assistance of the Monitors. He directly instructed the 6th and 7th grades, but was ultimately accountable for the successful education of all the students in the school.

Being a schoolmaster was a very honorable position. Mr. Taylor was employed by the Bahamian government, was educated of course, and as most educators worthy of their titles took very serious the calling to empower his pupils for their future success in life. Orthnell would become an example of such success. Even though he did not complete the 7th grade and graduate he was equipped with the necessary mathematics and language skills to eventually become an extremely articulate and successful businessman in the U.S. The monitors and Mr. Taylor served him well. He could not have achieved what he has without the education he received in the school in The Bight under Mr. Taylor's leadership.

The school building itself was like most buildings in Mastic Point: simple, wood-framed, with no electricity and no indoor plumbing. All grade levels were educated in this building. Each grade was grouped separately in the one room so that they could receive their instruction. Students would have to leave the building to go to the bathroom in the school's outhouse. Along with their very simple meals for lunch, students would also be given a vitamin and a little carnation milk for their health.

Along with schools, no other institutions outside of the family are as vital in most societies as the religious centers. In Andros there were a few Churches; all of them of course presided over by Black priests, pastors, or brothers. Church was vital to the people of Andros. There was an Anglican, Baptist, and Roman Catholic Church in Andros. Chef and his siblings all attended the

Catholic Church for services and Sunday School. Though there was not always a Priest present, a resident of Andros, Brother Francis who had come there from Nassau, facilitated services and Catholic education. Orthnell and all of his siblings were required to attend Mass every Sunday regardless if Rose attended or not, something she at times chose not to do.

Individuals like Brother Francis and Mr. Taylor, and even the young monitors were extremely important figures in the lives of the people of Andros and they loomed large in the psyches of those whose futures and intellectual and spiritual development were dependent on them. Young Orthnell was so impacted by these individuals that he remembers them vividly now at 82 and pays homage to them by stressing their roles and impact in his and so many others' lives. The value of these people in such vital leadership roles, running the institutions on which their society was built instilled in the youngsters of Andros a positive self-image and a belief in their potential.

Some other important figures in Orthnell's life in Andros were the "grannies". The grannies were the only doctors known to Orthnell as he grew up in Andros. The grannies were older women who attended to the health needs of the people. The grannies had no formal medical training, but instead relied on remedies and wisdom passed down through many generations. The grannies assisted in serious illnesses that people encountered and in the most important and sometimes dangerous life event of giving birth.

One event in Orthnell's life illustrates the importance and wisdom of the grannies. At 9 or 10 years old Orthnell developed a rash, was extremely weak, and had a severe fever that induced delirium. It was believed that he had typhus and was being attended to by his grandmother Elma. Out of concern for her grandson, Elma consulted one of the grannies. She was told to employ a medical strategy that was commonly used in treating serious fevers. For his fever Grandma Elma was told to wrap scolding hot hominy grits in a towel and wrap it around Orthnell's waist and send him to bed. This process was carried out a couple of times a day and within 2 days' time the fever broke and he recovered. No one can say for sure if it was the hot grits in the towel that restored Orthnell to health or not, or if he would have recovered on his own anyway. Perhaps it was simply the positive thinking and faith in the abilities of the grannies that strengthened the young man and helped him recover. Whatever it was, the grannies were able to advise people and made it so that they were not helpless in the face of sometimes very severe illnesses. It is important to note that Orthnell and others like him living on the Islands did not have vaccinations for the prevention of infectious diseases and modern treatments like antibiotics to treat illnesses. There was only the grannies and the traditional, natural remedies like the hot grits being tied around the waist and taking to the bed for a bad fever.

There is one realm where the Grannies had complete authority and that was when women were giving birth. Again, in the U.S. and other Western countries, midwives fulfilled this same purpose, and in many places were the sole experts on child birth up until recent times. When a grannie was called to the home for a delivery the she was given complete reign in the home during the labor and delivery. Children were most often told to leave the house and the labor and delivery would commence. Wonie Oliver was a prominent midwife that oversaw the birth of many of Orthnell's siblings and most likely his as well.

It is interesting to note that the grannies were not necessarily old women. In fact Wonie Oliver who died in 2010 at the age of 94 was in her 30s when Orthnell was a boy and already a grannie. Some of the other grannies in Mastic Point were Tracy Martin, Becky Martin, and Mary Pickstock. They too may have started in their vocation at young ages. Essentially it didn't matter the age of the grannies. What mattered was that they carried with them the knowledge and intuitive sense of what people needed and how to comfort them in their conditions and heal them.

Even the sawmill that provided many jobs for people on the islands of Andros was run by Blacks even though it was owned by Whites. Mr. Bettle, the owner, was the father of Ivory and Willie who were integral in the dreadful hunting story described earlier. The sawmill was managed by Blacks from the island and manned by Blacks as well, including Orthnell and other youngsters. Orthnell began working in the sawmill at 9-years-old. His job was to help "keep the dust down." As dust built up near the chains that ran the saws, Orthnell and others would use shovels to relieve the buildup and keep the paths of the chains clear and as cool as possible. It sounds like a frightening job, especially for adolescents, but it is no different from children working in mines and textiles before labor reforms in the West. In fact, one of Orthnell's close friends, Garnett Devo died at the mill, not in the process of keeping the dust down, but catching a nap near one of the huge tractors near the site. The tractors, which were used for multiple tasks stayed running almost constantly, were all around, and almost impossible to avoid. Garnett, being tired, decided to take a nap on one of his breaks. Being smaller, also about 9 or 10, he was positioned on the ground in what he though was a safe space, but near a tractor. Tragically, the operator, not noticing him, began to move the tractor backwards and rolled over Garnett. He had no chance of survival and died instantly. Just as in mining towns, the people of Mastic Point mourned collectively upon receiving the news of Garnett's death. In fact, Orthnell worked at the saw mill only about a week or two after Garnett's death, as the reality of the dangers of the mill and the memory of his friend proved too much.

He was paid about $3.50 a day. The sawmill was about 4 miles from Orthnell's home, in a place called San Andros, on the furthest edge of Mastic Point and as many as 10 men, young and old walked from near Orthnell's home to the mill with lunch pails in hand, filled with johnny cake, fruit, and perhaps some dried fish or other meat. Johnny cake was and is a staple food in the Bahamas. It is made from flour, water, and baking soda. It is an everyday bread, eaten with lunch or dinner, or as a snack. On a good day, a truck would pass by and some of them could jump on board and ride to the mill, sparing them the long walk. These trucks were the only motor vehicles that Orthnell encountered growing up. No one he knew had a car. Literally everyone walked to their destinations, and a few fortunate people had bikes to ride.

Thus far, I have described independent businessmen, educators, religious leaders, and medical providers, all of whom were Black. This may seem like a statement of the obvious but I believe it is vitally important to understanding the mindset of Orthnell when he made his decision to stow away and pursue a dream of living in the United States. In order to do great things one must have a positive self-image, not hampered by doubt and fear of the unknown. It is clear that growing up and not seeing a White person until he was 12 gave Orthnell a sense that as a Black man he could do anything he wanted to because he saw other Blacks, his neighbors, his relatives, his elders, fulfilling all of the essential roles in society. This same reality probably contributed to the success of many of his siblings as well. For instance, his older brother Henderson became a master builder. He never received formal schooling for his trade, but served as an apprentice to skilled carpenters and builders on the Islands. Today, there are numerous homes and buildings throughout Andros and elsewhere in the Bahamas that he built. Seeing Black men and women be successful without much if any interference by or help from Whites gave Orthnell and others like him, even if the others didn't leave the Bahamas, the confidence to branch out and do whatever they wanted to do. It gave Orthnell especially a boldness and a sense of invincibility that compelled him to leave the Bahamas and come to the United States to fulfill his dreams.

Orthnell at 13 or 14.

THE URGE TO LEAVE

After living 13 years in Mastic Point, Orthnell began to feel that he wanted to leave. It seems awfully early in life to make such a serious decision, but he made it. Perhaps it was the hard work, either retrieving water and wood, or perhaps his experience of working in the sawmill or being slapped with a wet rope by his uncle Lar. More than likely, all these things factored into Orthnell's decision to venture out and leave his home, but there was something else as well. Orthnell had become accustomed to hearing tales from men in his community who had left and gone to America to do seasonal work, mostly in Florida and other areas where farmers needed laborers. These men talked about the opportunities in America as well as the luxuries that were there; luxuries like cars in a place where no one had one, and the only motor vehicles anyone saw were carrying lumber and supplies to a sawmill. These tales must have done quite a number on Orthnell's young imagination and had a profound effect on his youthful aspirations. Whatever it was, he made up his mind and began planning to first leave Andros and then the Bahamas all together.

His strategy was to scout out the boats that were going to and from Nassau. He spent several days watching, studying times, and the behavior of crews, until finally he realized his best opportunity. He would climb aboard a steam ship called the *Ms. Holland* under the cover of darkness. The *Ms. Holland* hauled lumber from the very mill in Andros where he had worked to Nassau.

Once aboard Orthnell made his way to the hull of the ship and hid behind a large steel beam that was near the engine room. He took nothing with him, except the clothes he was wearing, and had no money. He made himself as comfortable as possible and waited a few hours for the ship to pull off at daybreak and thus began his trip off the Island of Andros.

The trip from Andros to Nassau was only about 2 hours, but once he arrived in Nassau, he again had to wait for nightfall to disembark for fear of being spotted. After being on the *Ms. Holland* for almost a full day, he was obviously hungry and tired. He had also become quite seasick which was unusual for him. He attributes this to the fact that he had never been on a motorized boat before, steam or otherwise. The *Ms. Holland* was a steam ship and quite different from the row boats and sailing vessels he had been on. Nevertheless, when nightfall came, he got off and was now in Nassau.

Now that he had landed in Nassau, young Orthnell set out to find someone he knew. He had several relatives who lived in Nassau, but he had no idea where they lived or how to locate them. As he walked around downtown Nassau he eventually found someone he recognized from Andros and asked where Charlotte, his first cousin lived. It happened that it was not far and he was able to walk there. When he arrived, of course, it was the middle of the night and no one was expecting him. Not only that, but Charlotte's house was filled to capacity. She had several children, lived in a small house, and all the beds and floor space were taken. After greeting his cousins, Orthnell went and slept on the front porch.

The idea of a young 13-year-old sleeping outdoors on a front porch seems cruel if not inhumane. However, when one factors in the climate and the fact that Orthnell was accustomed to sleeping on floors which was common, especially for children. Even in Rose's home, Orthnell and his siblings simply slept on the floor atop blankets for a bit of comfort and their hands placed together between their legs or bent underneath their heads for a type of pillow. Also, it is important to keep in mind that this was part of the sacrifice that Orthnell decided to make and it most assuredly would not be the last.

Orthnell remained with Charlotte's family for several days, ate well, rested up, and planned his next move. Little did he know, word had gotten to Rose back in Andros, and she sent Henderson, now 17, to get his little brother. He sailed to Nassau aboard a fishing boat that was captained by Austin Rolle, Orthnell and Henderson's great uncle by marriage. Austin was married to

Grandmother Elma's sister Minnie. Once Henderson found Orthnell at Charlotte's house, he immediately scolded him about his inconsiderate indiscretion and the anguish he was causing his mother. "How you get to Nassau, boy?!" he asked him in anger. He even slapped him around, something that was not completely unknown to Orthnell as Henderson often took on the role of guardian in not only Orthnell's life, but the life of Rose's other children as well. In fact, it was a constant reality that in the absence of a father figure, as the oldest brother, Henderson was to be respected as a father, and possessed much of the authority typically afforded the male heads of household.

So, with a couple of slaps and strong words, Henderson and Orthnell boarded Austin Rolle's boat to return home to Andros. The trip was now a full day's journey instead of the 2 hours is took Orthnell to go to Nassau. The *Ms. Holland* was powered by a steam engine, unlike Uncle Austin's sailboat. Once on the sailboat and heading safely back to Andros, Henderson continued to try and encourage Orthnell's obedience to him and his mother, urging him that "if you leave the island again, I better be with you." Again, emphasis is placed on the role of Henderson as guardian, and the reality that he would be the one to safely bring Orthnell to Nassau, if he was to come at all. This event, the scolding, the discipline by his brother, the embarrassment of failing to carry out his plan of leaving for a more permanent stent, left a bitter taste in Orthnell's mouth and only fueled his desire to ultimately leave Andros for good, and try his hand at life somewhere else. Thus, he began planning his next "escape" from his home island.

Once he was back in Andros, Orthnell spent time telling stories of his adventure: his success at stowing away, what he saw in Nassau, his encounter with his brother, and the sailboat ride back home. His relationship with Rose was affected to some degree, but Rose had some inkling long before this time that this type of problem or something similar was going to occur. When he was six years old she told him "you're my son and I'm never going to get to know you." At the time the 6-year-old Orthnell did not know what to make of this, but now as he looks back, it makes absolute sense. Actually, the prophecy could have even more implications. Namely, that at the heart of Orthnell's desire and willingness to leave his mother without notice and for long periods of time was a lack of a sense of obligation to her in that way. Even now, he does not regret or consider very seriously the effects on Rose or anyone else that may have been negatively affected by his venturing spirit. To him, then and now, he holds the burden he felt to leave his home above all else, and likens it to a divine or spiritual calling that supplanted any familial obligations that he might have otherwise allowed to guide his life.

As time went on, Orthnell returned to his fishing and crabbing and spending time with his siblings. He also returned to the courtship of a young woman named Sally who he had attended school with and lived close to. Sally was very attractive. Her skin was "fair" or light, although there was not much distinction made between people of different hues in Orthnell's community. His "romance" with Sally was innocent. The times they spent together were at Sally's house, as he was not allowed to take her out alone. He recalls visiting her several times, sitting on her couch with her mother between the two of them as they exchanged words and smiles. His relationship with Sally would be another one affected by him leaving the island. In fact, once he left for good, eventually making it to the United States, he saw Sally only one time after that.

He also found work. He was hired by great uncle Austin to cook for him and his crew aboard his fishing boat. The boat went out for about one month at a time, fishing for sponge, conch, and other sea life. It was equipped with a live well to keep the catch fresh, and as long as the haul was sufficient, Orthnell got paid. Uncle Austin's expectation was for Orthnell to prepare several meals a day as the men were out at sea. Each day he lit a fire on the deck to prepare meals which consisted of things such as stew conch, pigeon peas and rice, and of course fried fish. The cooking was done on the open deck on a "fire half" which was basically a wood fire on a bed of sand and rock.

Orthnell enjoyed his days aboard the boat greatly and looks back on them with fondess. The crew got along well and were nice to him. Much of the time, when not engaged in spearing sponge or catching conch, was spent telling stories, singing spiritual and calypso songs like "Joe Billy," and even dancing. Lacking any forms of electronic entertainment, radios especially, the men relied on each other and their various gifts to joyfully pass the time, whether it was telling tales of the past or present, or offering renditions of popular songs. It is no wonder that Chef Alfredo is extremely adept at telling stories and has an extremely engaging personality. Such qualities were honed in environments where individuals' natural gifts are so crucial to day to day life.

Making a living for the men on Austin Rolle's boat was no easy task, and Orthnell was right in the thick of this hard work with them. The sailboat was only the vessel that the men used to get to a location that was ripe for good fishing or sponging (Captain Rolle had a crew of 5, not including Orthnell who was not considered technically a part of the crew). They rowed two dinghies that were tied to the side of the sailboat to a spot that they believed was ripe for fishing and try for a haul. The crew would split up and go out in the dinghies to fish. Then they used a water glass like Orthnell used as a youngster to peer down into the water to locate fish and sponge. Once the right spot was designated, the fishing and sponging commenced. The men would stay out on the dinghies for 2 or 3 hours and then return to the main boat. As stated before, they usually stayed out at sea for about a month. What really determined the duration was the catch. They wouldn't return to land unless the live well was full.

Once the live well was full Captain Rolle guided the boat to Nassau where the men disembarked and sold what they caught. There were many more merchants and places to sell what they caught and get paid there than back in Andros. Once all of their catch was sold they returned home to their wives and families. It was an exciting time. They had been out at sea for several weeks and they came back with money to support their loved ones. After being home for a while the men prepared to go back to sea. This time, Orthnell would not be with them though. He never left Nassau and didn't go with the men home to see his mother or family. According to him, what he wanted was closer to Nassau than Andros, so he stayed.

Ironically, it was not cooking aboard Austin Rolle's fishing boat where Orthnell was set on the path to becoming a culinary expert. It was his time spent at a Roman Catholic Monastery that did that for him, though cooking on Austin Rolle's boat may have been a sign of what was to come. Once he was in Nassau, Orthnell again began to search for relatives, not the same ones though. He was now looking for one special relative: his father, Joshua, who he'd never seen. As he walked about Nassau he spotted a young man from Andros named Creswell Munnings. Creswell was able to help Orthnell find where Joshua lived, but he also gave Orthnell information about a possible opportunity for him. You see, Creswell was studying to be a Roman Catholic Brother at St. Augustine's Monastery in an area called Fox Hill in Nassau which was about 10 miles from where he was, and also about 10 miles from where his father lived. But, before he pursued the possibility of joining the monastery he needed to meet his father.

Creswell did not know exactly where Joshua lived, but he was able to point Orthnell in a general direction. That direction was "over the hill". "Over the hill" was generally understood to be where the natives, the Blacks lived. "In front of the hill" was where the Whites, the "guana" as they are called lived. Once he went "over the hill" he was able to ask around and find Joshua's house. "He lives on Westley Corner, 4th house from the corner, on the left," one of the natives told him. When he got to the door, anxiety filled him, and all at once, the reality of meeting his father made him extremely nervous. He knocked on the door and a woman answered. It was Lolitta, his father's wife. "Who are you?" "What do you want?" Lolitta said. "Does Mr. Russell live here?" Orthnell replied. Lolitta continued, "Yes, but he's at work." "Who are you?" "I'm his son from Andros." Lolitta was somewhat excited and invited Orthnell in to wait for Joshua to come home. Apparently, Joshua had spoken about Orthnell before and Lolitta knew that her husband had a son she (and he) had never met. It took a couple of hours, but finally Joshua arrived, and to his surprise his son was sitting in his house, and he laid eyes on him for the first time in his life.

The first encounter with his father was awkward. The two shook hands. There was no hug or embrace, just a manly handshake. Joshua proceeded to ask Orthnell "what you doing up here?" "I'm here to see you." And thus began the process of catching up on years of life that Joshua had not been a part of. Joshua agreed to allow Orthnell to stay in his home while he was in Nassau, provided that he did not go and come whenever he wanted; essentially Joshua wanted him to respect his house. Orthnell ended up staying for about 3 months with Joshua and Lolitta and their 2 children, Orthnell's half siblings, Henry and Nettie.

THE MONASTIC LIFE

While living with his family in Nassau Orthnell tried his hand at a few jobs: grocery delivery boy, shoe shine boy, assisting Joshua's brother Stanley who was a brick mason. Working with Stanley was physically demanding to say the least, and something he did not want to do for long. There was no idle time for the young man in pursuit of a dream. After doing these jobs he decided to visit the monastery where Creswell was living and studying. So, he made the 10-mile walk to Fox Hill and there he met Father Frederick, who ran St. Augustine's. When asked, Orthnell did not hide the fact that he had run away from home, and instead told the father exactly what his status was. To his surprise, Father Frederick did not view this as a reason to deny him the opportunity to stay. He did comment that "you are mighty young." And, "you cannot stay with the brothers." "You must stay downstairs in a room by yourself." This was fine with Orthnell. He had gone from stowing away on a steamboat, to sleeping on a porch, and then from Charlotte's house to Joshua's. He was now being offered the opportunity to have his own space, his own bed, a bit of privacy and solitude. However, he was told that he would not be able to attend the monastery school where Creswell was attending because of his age. Creswell was a couple of years older than Orthnell. Instead, he would have to attend St. Anselm School which was nearby and offered local youth education beyond the primary grades, which he did gladly.

In addition to attending school daily, Orthnell was given chores as well. Among them was milking 5 goats that were maintained on the premises and assisting the head chef, Mr. Ferguson. Of course, he also was obligated to pray every day, four times to be exact. Mr. Ferguson was a large, dark-skinned Bahamian who was quite adroit in the kitchen. Orthnell assisted him is the preparation of 3 meals each day for themselves and the 10 men that were either brothers already or were studying to be brothers like Creswell.

For breakfast Orthnell assisted in preparing such things as omelets, fried bacon, ham, fried fish, and grits. Lunch would often include a variety of different sandwiches, among them was the famous Reuben, salads, boiled fish, and johnny cake. And, for dinner he would help prepare things such as lamb chops, steak, and fish. It is clear that the fare that was being prepared and served at St. Augustine's was better than an average Bahamian would be eating on a daily basis. Finding a home at the Monastery was the first in a series of fortunate events in young Orthnell's life.

Not only was he eating well, being educated, and experiencing a level of privacy and solitude that he had never had, he was also learning the skills of a chef and as he explains it, it was at St. Augustine's, working alongside Mr. Ferguson that he began to feel that he was "born to cook". He and Mr. Ferguson would prepare each meal and carry them to the dining room. Before eating, all the men had to go to the sanctuary and pray.

At St. Augustine's Sunday was a big day for Orthnell and the other men. They would rise early, about 6 o'clock, and attend private mass for themselves that lasted 2 to 3 hours. It consisted of them praying and going to confession. They would then have breakfast, followed by another mass that consisted of hymns and a liturgy. The services were private. The men lived and worshiped together, serving God as one. Chef recalls how he as a young man developed friendships with the men at St. Augustine's and how significant a part of his development this was. As he looks back on his experiences, many of which would not have happened without his faith in God and himself, he recalls his time at the Monastery as part of the bedrock from which the rest of his life was built.

The men he met at the Monastery had a profound impact on him. Mr. Ferguson, of course, having taught him some of the finer points of the culinary arts, and Father Frederick opening the Monastery to him in the first place, but also the other men as well, helped him to see the potential that men like him had. He recalls all of the men there being kind and treating him like a younger brother. Some of them were funny and like the men on the fishing boat, they were engaging, and very good story tellers.

Despite the fact that Orthnell, now 14, enjoyed being at St. Augustine's he realized that he did not want to stay there and pursue a life as a brother or a priest, so he began to prepare to return to Nassau after about 7 months. He appreciated the discipline, the cultivation of a spiritual life, and the fellowship with the other men, but he felt that his calling in life was something different, something beyond the walls of the monastery. Something that also contributed to Orthnell's decision was his friend Creswell's decision to also leave the monastery. He wasn't sure why Creswell left, but his friend's decision helped him to initiate his own departure. He discussed his desire to leave with Father Frederick, and without pressuring him, Father Frederick bid him farewell. Orthnell said goodbye to the men of the monastery and left for Nassau and his father's house.

THE QUEEN OF NASSAU

Orthnell returned to Joshua and Lolitta's house where he began planning his next move. What he knew was that if he had any hope of leaving the Bahamas and one day making it to America he was going to have to do something pretty spectacular. With very little money and no sanctioning by his parents he was going to have to stow away and plan the whole thing on his own, but first he would spend some time working, and getting acquainted with the world of the docks and life on the sea. To put himself in a strategic location for boarding a ship he built a shoeshine box, filled it with leather cleaners, polishes, cloths, and brushes, and began shining shoes down at the docks in Nassau. He would also go door to door and to various professional offices to shine shoes. He was able to begin saving money that he would need when he ended up in the U.S.

One day, while he was shining shoes on the docks the captain of the cruise ship *Queen of Nassau*, passed by. Orthnell yelled out "hey capitan, you want your shoes shined?" "Maybe when I come back," he replied. On his way back toward his ship he did stop for a shoe shine. As his good fortune would have it the captain invited Orthnell aboard the ship to shine the mates' shoes as well. Orthnell, with a mind toward his ultimate plan, jumped at this opportunity. He really wanted to take things a step further and asked the captain for a permanent job on the ship. "Boy, you pretty young ain't you," the captain retorted. "I am,"

Orthnell responded but added "I'm a hard worker." In turn the captain asked "do you have a passport?" Orthnell did not and felt a serious sense of dissuasion, but was determined to not give up. The conversation between him and the captain ended with some ambivalence, but Orthnell decided that with his introduction to the captain, his proposition about working, and the captain's question about his passport that there was hope. He would do everything in his power to get his passport and be ready when he approached the captain again, something he was definitely going to do. It helped also that his old friend Creswell, after leaving the St. Augustine's Monastery landed a job on the *Queen of Nassau* as well.

The process of getting his passport took 2 to 3 months. Something that made this process difficult was the fact that Orthnell did not have a birth certificate. The only official record of his existence was a baptism record that was held at the church where he was baptized. However, with the help of a family friend by the name of Mrs. Knowles, a friend of Joshua and Lolitta's, who worked at the American Consulate, he received his passport. Once he had it, he went back to the docks to wait for the *Queen of Nassau*. When it docked, it took 3 or 4 days before Orthnell and the captain's paths crossed again. This time he would be prepared though. It worked, and the captain invited him aboard the ship. He did have to wait though. The ship would go out and come back in a matter of 2 to 3 weeks, then he could join the crew, a wait he didn't mind.

In the meantime, Orthnell continued to shine shoes and save up his money. At home his relationship with Lolitta grew more than with Joshua, just by virtue of Lolitta being conversational, and Joshua being very quiet and non-engaging, at least with his son. Joshua generally held the view shared by some other men that children were not to be joked with, played with, or otherwise positively engaged by adults. As a result, the only engagement that Orthnell had with his father was when he felt the need to correct him about something or give him a directive. A common adage of the time was "If you play with a puppy he will kick you in the mouth." Essentially, too much interaction with children could eventually lead to disrespect.

More than likely, Joshua's disinterest in his son, at least as far as Orthnell knew, added to Orthnell's desire to leave and go to America. He had no true emotional ties to his father. He loved his mother, but didn't mind being away from her for extended periods of time. He resented the disciplinarian role of his brother Henderson. Opportunities were limited and life was hard in the islands. With all of this, leaving for America couldn't happen fast enough.

Orthnell had several different jobs aboard the *Queen of Nassau*. His first job was as a switchboard operator. Next, he was a bedroom steward. Finally, he was a doorman in the ship's dining room. He had no particular preference for the jobs he was assigned to do. He was just happy to be working. At 14, he was the youngest member of the ship's crew and earning good money, $25.00 a week. He also was getting the chance to see the world, at least the Caribbean world. He travelled to Jamaica, Haiti, and the Dominican Republic. By far, his favorite place to visit was Cuba. He recalls the women of Cuba being extremely beautiful and the environment, especially Havana, exciting and full of life.

It was on his travels throughout the Caribbean that Orthnell had his first sexual encounters. In fact, he began to really enjoy the seemingly unlimited access to women for hire. Being only 14 and having money to spend, he became adept at buying sex. In fact, he did so in all of the islands he ventured to. Creswell, his buddy and former brother in training also enjoyed buying sex from women in the islands and often times they would go together, approach the "overseers" or pimps and make their selections. Orthnell was truly living a grown man's life at this point. He was aided greatly by his height and maturity. Rarely was he asked about his age. He navigated freely in the worlds in which he traveled, and did virtually whatever he wanted and had the money to do.

Orthnell's education while working on the Queen of Nassau extended to other areas as well. Among them was gambling. He rolled his first pair of dice on the cruise liner. He also learned the deferential treatment that was to be extended to the White passengers. His communication with most of the passengers, Europeans, Canadians, and some Americans, was limited to "yes sir," "no sir," "yes ma'am," and "no ma'am." Not that he wouldn't have referred to the individuals responsible for him having a job this way anyhow, and not that he hadn't grown up referring to his elders that way, but there was clearly a significant line between those who had the means to travel on such cruise lines, and those who could only work on them. Later in life, when Orthnell became an entrepreneur, the respectful deference that he learned as a young man carried over into his businesses and his compelling need to treat customers with the utmost respect, making them feel as if they are indeed his number one concern. So, it wasn't necessarily a negative thing that he "catered" to the White passengers that he served. It was this experience that made him an expert in customer etiquette and a successful restaurateur.

Orthnell completed two voyages working aboard the Queen of Nassau lasting about 3 weeks each. After the second voyage he returned to Nassau to Joshua's house. Once he was back in Nassau he again found work at the docks: he helped people clean fish, carry packages, and yes, took up his shoe shine business again.

He also entered his first significant romantic relationship. The woman was Alfreda, an older woman, 22 with 2 kids. Even though Orthnell was mature for his age, he still was not quite prepared for the ordeal that "Freda" would take him through. As a mature woman with a small family, Freda offered Orthnell some stability in his already very transitory life. As he recalls, Freda was petite, of medium build, and very beautiful. After a few visits and time spent with Freda, Orthnell "was in love." He began to make a point to go and visit Freda whenever he had the chance and when he wasn't working at the docks. On one such occasion, however, he was dreadfully shocked when he found another man at Freda's house. Apparently, Orthnell was beat out by an older man. He was devastated and it would be many years before Orthnell would lend his heart to a woman as he had done with Freda. He did learn a valuable lesson about love though: the potential is always there for some pain.

All of his adventures aboard the *Queen of Nassau* and in the Caribbean served to increase Orthnell's confidence in himself and knowledge of what lay beyond his home country. For a teenage young man that essentially saw himself as too big for a small island country he was sharpening his sense of the possibilities in life. It wouldn't be long before he would make his way to the States. He didn't go there permanently at first and didn't stow away just yet. He first took advantage of an opportunity to go to the states as a migrant farm worker.

A MIGRANT WORKER

Sometime before his 15th birthday Orthnell was presented with an opportunity to go to the States on a contract to work on farms in Florida for one year. Orthnell knew for years that Bahamians were sometimes contracted by the U.S. Government to migrate seasonally to work, but he didn't know anyone first-hand who did this and that could help him do it. That all changed when his Uncle William, Rose's brother, decided to migrate on such a contract. When Orthnell heard that his Uncle would be going to the States he asked him if he could go. "You're too young!" William replied. This was something that Orthnell had become accustomed to hearing by this point, but paid no attention to. Orthnell knew that these contracts were facilitated by "bosses" or men whose business it was to locate laborers in the islands and arrange for their passage to the U.S., and placement on farms. "Let the boss say that." Orthnell replied. With that, William arranged for Orthnell to meet the boss who he was working with.

Upon meeting the boss, Orthnell, exuding the confidence that he had learned had the potential to produce positive outcomes, approached the boss and asked him if he could go to work in America. "You sure you want to do that?" is the response he received. "Yes, sir," Orthnell replied. Looking back and evaluating that very important question that the boss asked him, and more importantly, his response is something that Orthnell would do continuously

33

once the boss agreed to take him and he found himself on various farms in Florida. The contract ended up being for only 6 months and all told there would be 20 Bahamians that would make the trip under contract. They flew together on Mackey Airlines (no longer in existence) and landed in Ft. Lauderdale.

This would be Orthnell's first plane ride. It was quite amazing and frightening for him all at once. It helped that his Uncle William was right there with him, and before he knew it, the plane was descending in the land where he ultimately wanted to be.

Once in Ft. Lauderdale, each of the contracted workers were distributed based on need. Orthnell ended up being designated for a farm in Homestead, Florida where he would go to help harvest tomatoes, beans, cabbages, and onions. His uncle, to his dismay, was sent to another location. This would be the last time that he would see William in Florida. They would reunite back home a year or so later when William's contract expired and Orthnell had returned as well. Nevertheless, he was in the U.S. and eager to see what it had to offer. Now, he had never done any farm work, so this whole experience was a leap in the dark, and it wouldn't be long before the harshness and monotony of the farm work would begin to weigh on him.

Once he was assigned to a particular farm, Orthnell boarded a truck and headed there. Once there, he was assigned a bunk in a dormitory type structure with several other men who he did not know and were from all different locations. A couple were from the Bahamas, but most were from elsewhere in the Caribbean, South America, and places in the U.S. The next morning all the men rose at 6:00 AM, ate a modest breakfast, and headed to the fields. Once he laid eyes on the fields Orthnell began to gain an idea of what was in store and how he greatly underestimated the severity of the work he had signed up for. His first task was to pick tomatoes of which there were acres upon acres. According to him the fields on the farm stretched for miles, "as far as the eye could see." And all his eyes could see was tomatoes. Every direction he turned, there was nothing but tomatoes. As he and the other men worked under the grueling sun, stopping only for lunch at noon, Orthnell's opinion of farm work and that life was that it was not for him.

After several days of working in the fields, Orthnell approached the manager of the operation where he was and told him that he didn't like the work. "You can't go home," was the retort. Perhaps it was his youth that made him think that he would receive some sympathy from the manager, but he received none. All of the men that Orthnell was working and living with in the barracks were older. Perhaps they were used to this work. Perhaps they had families to support and could not spare the energy required to think about their condition as they thought about making money to send to their families back home. Whatever the case, Orthnell felt alone and grew more and more miserable as the days went by. In fact, he eventually went to the manager again to complain, and again he received the same reply. After about four instances of complaining, the manager agreed to transfer him to a different farm.

This time he would be placed on a citrus farm in Leesburg where he would be used to harvest oranges and grapefruits. The problem now was that in order to harvest the fruits he had to climb trees, some of which were between 18 and 20 feet high. He never was required to go to the top and "pick ceiling," but he saw men do it and the whole process, high or low, was not to his liking. It wasn't long before he began to despise this work just as he had the row crops on the Homestead farm. And again he complained to the manager. It was a different manager and a different farm, but the answer again was "you cannot go home."

Orthnell was transferred to a farm in Belle Glade, that grew among other things, celery, lettuce, and corn. This farm was extremely swampy and humid. Orthnell spent much of his time behind a mule-powered machine that harvested celery. Between the climate and trudging along behind a mule all day, after about 2 months, Orthnell had enough reason to complain to the manager once again. He had stayed on the Belle Glade farm longer than any other farm, but he eventually tired of that work too. "Ok. Russell, perhaps you will like the sugar cane farm." Once again, a manager in an attempt to satisfy Orthnell who at this point was about 4 months into his contract moved him to a different farm. The sugar cane farm was in Clewiston, about 20 miles from Belle Glade, so not far away. The work was quite different, and Orthnell found it to be the least desirable of all the farm work he had done so far.

On the sugar cane farm, Orthnell was employed in torching the cane fields, something that was done to kill the weeds and drive out rattlesnakes. After only a few days of being in the cane fields and seeing men become blackened with soot, Orthnell became very ill with the flu. He had to be taken to a local hospital where he remained for one and a half weeks recovering. It is most likely a number of factors that contributed to Orthnell becoming ill. Naturally, the new environment and exposure to new germs could have made him susceptible to serious illness. Also, the stress of the labor he was being required to do. It is also likely that the sheer misery that had set in on him contributed to him falling ill. Whatever the cause, he was sicker than he had ever been, and now desperate to find a way out of his predicament.

As a contract worker the only way for Orthnell to be taken back home was once his contract was fulfilled. He still had over a month left on his contract, so if he wanted to return home he would have to find and fund his own way. Even with the changes from one farm to the other Orthnell had made enough money to afford a Greyhound bus ticket out of Belle Glade and a plane ticket back to Nassau. So, he took the bus back to Ft. Lauderdale and then flew back to Nassau, knowing that farm work would not be his ticket to a good life in America.

STOWING AWAY

Once he returned to Nassau, he went and spent some time in Andros, re-uniting with his mother and family, and planning his ultimate feat of stow-ing away to America on his own. He didn't stay very long in Andros before making his way back to Nassau and work on the docks.

He continued to shine shoes, eventually being allowed to come aboard the *Evangeline*, a cruise ship that docked in Nassau once a month before leaving for the States, stopping first in Miami. Orthnell would come aboard when the *Evangeline* was docked and shine the shoes of the crew and pas-sengers. As he became comfortable with walking around the big cruise ship yelling "shoe shine boy, shoe shine?" he began to search for a secluded spot on the ship where he could hide and make his secret journey. He found such a place in the ship's bow. It took several days for him to have his space in the bow ready for his journey. He went to a room aboard the *Evangeline* and took bed linens and put them into his secret spot for comfort. He also stocked up on foods like bread, dried fish, johnny cake, and fruit. It wouldn't be an extremely long trip, but Orthnell didn't know what he would need once he reached Florida or how long he would have to stay on the boat be-fore it would be safe to get off.

Once his hidden area was prepared, Orthnell was ready to make his trip. He told no one about his intentions and to his family, Joshua and Lolitta and their children, this was just another day that Orthnell was going to the docks to work. He wore jeans and a tee shirt, socks and shoes, and had $10.00 in his pocket when he went aboard the *Evangeline* and didn't come off. The horn sounded once and then a double sounding as it always did. The only difference this time was that it was carrying some unchecked cargo. Orthnell was off to America and his new life.

Orthnell had not told anyone goodbye because he had not told anyone he was leaving, including Joshua or Rose. He was so committed to leaving the Bahamas that he did not want to jeopardize his plans by having someone stop him as Henderson did when he came to Nassau to bring him back to Andros over a year earlier. One of the recurring themes in Orthnell's life is a detachment from personal relationships, even the most intimate ones like between him and his mother or his siblings. These connections had the potential of holding him back or causing him to doubt his objectives. So, he made such crucial decisions like stowing away and leaving his home and family without a word and with no regrets.

The *Evangeline* took half the day to get to Miami. Orthnell knew when the ship had docked, because he could feel the swaying of the ship stop. He couldn't hear much from where he was, so he simply had to wait until enough time had lapsed, allowing most of the passengers and crew to disembark. According to him, he was relying on the Spirit of God to give him direction. Once he was on deck he felt led to grab one of several suitcases that he saw that had not been claimed or removed yet and walk off the ship. This seems to have been a good move as he made it off the ship without being stopped. He walked past the immigration officers that he saw and two police officers on horseback, but none questioned him or tried to stop him. He continued walking and eventually crossed Biscayne Boulevard where he stopped a White man and asked "where are the colored people in Miami?" The man in turn asked Orthnell "where you from?" Something (again, he believes it was the Spirit of God) told him to say "I'm from Carolina," which he did. Orthnell had never been to North or South Carolina, and didn't know why he felt moved to say that, but he did, and it worked. It must have been the Spirit again. "Just go across the railroad tracks," the man responded, and Orthnell was off to find some people who looked like him and might be able to help him.

To his great surprise, once Orthnell made it across the tracks and walked around for a couple of hours he ran into a man from Andros named Percy

Marshall. "Slim! Man it's good to see you!" said Percy as he walked over and embraced him. He didn't know how or why Percy had ended up in Miami. He was just glad to see a familiar face. Percy proceeded to inquire about Orthnell being in Miami and again Orthnell fabricated saying "some people from Jacksonville brought me here and I'm looking for my cousin." Even though he was looking for his cousin, Orthnell did not want to reveal the truth about how he made it to Miami for fear of it getting back to his family in the Bahamas. "Who's your cousin?" responded Percy. "Louise Russell." Louise was Orthnell's first cousin. However, all that he knew was that she lived in Miami. He had never seen her before and knew very little about her. "I know Louise Russell!" said Percy. At this point Orthnell realized that it must be destiny for him to be on the journey he was on as things amazingly unfolded for him. Percy continued: "she lives on 8th Avenue." Percy agreed to take him to where Louise lived which was several blocks away.

When Percy and Orthnell arrived at Louise's house and after Orthnell explained who he was, he found out that he couldn't stay with Louise because she had a crowded house, Percy, recognizing the dilemma that Orthnell was faced with, told him "you can stay with me, but you will have to sleep on the floor," something that was no problem for Orthnell. So, off to Percy's house they went.

Percy lived on 4th Avenue with his mother, father, and sister. Orthnell discovered that the entire family immigrated to Miami a couple of years earlier to find work. They originally came on farm contracts and stayed after they expired. Having been in Florida much longer than him, they were essential to helping him find his way to a job and some stability. After only being there a day or so, he asked Percy where he could find some work. Almost immediately, Percy showed Orthnell how to get around and where he might have some luck finding a job. It was up to Orthnell now to navigate Miami on foot and the public busses.

His first trip on the bus was one that he'll never forget. Not knowing the social order or understanding the system of segregation that was in place he sat down on a seat in the front of the bus. Immediately, an older black woman from a little further back gently called to him and waved him back to her. Orthnell got up and went to the woman. "Where you from?" she said and again the response: "I'm from Carolina." Surely this must have raised some red flags for the woman, but she had no reason to be too concerned about who Orthnell was or why he was in Miami. She simply responded "colored people can't sit in the front of the bus." "You don't know that?" If Orthnell was from Carolina there was no way that he would not have known such a basic fact. But, the woman had no reason to be suspicious of Orthnell, so they just rode along to their destination.

Orthnell managed to make it to Miami Beach where he began his search for work and fortunately landed a job. His first job would be at a Caribbean theater as a custodian. There was an obstacle to his employment though. He had no Florida I.D. To get one he would have to go to a local police station, which he did. Surprisingly, he was able to get the I.D., even without documentation of his legal status. He was able to get one at the local motor vehicles office. It cost him a few dollars which he was happy to pay. He was able to use Percy's address as his place of residence, and having sat for a photo, he was on his way.

Orthnell worked at the theater and continued to live with Percy and his family until the following November and then he planned his next move. It was 1955 and Orthnell was now 16. He had heard from some of the men who had left the Bahamas for work and travelled to New York City, that that was where true opportunities were. They came back home with money and tales of excitement which were vivid in young Orthnell's mind. He thought that in New York "money grew on trees." So, with some of the money he was able to save up he bought a used grey suit from a second-hand shop and a bus ticket to New York. Once he returned to Percy's house he told his hosts that he would be leaving. To them it must have been curious that a teenager who they knew was in Miami alone and now headed to the largest city in the U.S., with seemingly no clear idea of what he would do and very few possessions, but there was nothing that they could do. Some would wonder why Percy's family didn't try to contact someone, Rose or some other relatives of Orthnell's to notify them that he was there and what he was planning, but they didn't. Perhaps it was the time period or maybe the culture. Whatever it was the Marshalls were there to help their young guest and didn't stand in his way.

On the day that he left, in late November, Orthnell put on his new suit, grabbed his suitcase that contained the few other clothes that he had, walked to the Greyhound station, and boarded a bus going north. Along with his few possessions and the money he had saved from his job at the Caribbean theater, he also had little knowledge of what a northern route in the U.S. was going to have in store for him.

NEW YORK CITY

As he travelled north, Orthnell noticed that it got progressively colder. It took over 24 hours and the hundreds of miles he traversed took him from the warm climates that he knew all of his life to a cold one that he was totally unprepared for. His bus stopped near Grand Central Station at about 9:00 PM. When he got off the bus, he felt what to him was arctic air passing through the fibers of his new suit. To him it was as though he was standing on 42nd Street completely naked! Even though it was only November and bound to get even colder, it was enough for Orthnell to realize he had greatly underestimated the challenges of his trip. He decided to go into Grand Central and sit down for a while. After getting up the courage to go out and face the intense cold, he went out onto the street again, watched others waiving their hand to hail a cab, and he eventually did the same, having no idea where the cab would take him. He shivered as he waited for a cab, but he soon would get one, warm up, and be on his way, wherever that would be.

"Where you going?" asked the cab driver. "Take me to a cheap motel." For some reason the cabbie drove Orthnell to the Hotel Theresa, the famous Harlem hotel. He didn't know any better so he got out, went in, and asked for a room. He was given a small room that he could only afford to stay two nights. After the second night he found a boarding house on 128th Street where he would live for most of his time in Harlem. It was one room in a brownstone managed by a woman named Ms. Roberts and cost $7.00 a day. It was clean, warm, and very basic, and Orthnell made it his home. Essentially he would only be sleeping there as most of his waking hours would be spent first finding work and then working to pay for his new life in the "Big Apple".

Once he got settled in the rooming house, he asked someone on the street where there was a secondhand store where he could go and buy some clothes suitable for the cold climate. He went and purchased a coat, hat, scarf, gloves, and boots. Now that he had the necessary gear for the New York weather he went to find work. As he started out it began to snow lightly. This was the first time that Orthnell had ever seen snow in person and he was amazed. The only other time he had seen snow was in a motion picture in a theater in Nassau when he was there living with Lolitta and Joshua. In awe, he stretched out his hand, letting the snow fall into it and melt. As he watched the melting snow he thought for a moment of how miraculous it was that he was in New York City. He considered briefly all of the people he left at home who may never see what he was seeing and experience life outside of the islands. He didn't dwell in that place too long. Time was of the essence and if he planned on staying in New York he was going to have to get a job.

The first day of looking produced no results. So, he set out again. This time he took a bus towards Midtown Manhattan. His search eventually led him to the Park Lane Hotel near Central Park. They had posted a sign that they needed a dishwasher in their restaurant. Orthnell applied, went through a brief interview with the manager, and was hired on the spot. He began working that day. He was able to put in about 6 hours before the restaurant closed. After work he took a bus back uptown to Harlem.

Orthnell reported faithfully to work every day, but something unexpected happened. He became very sick. It is not that Orthnell was invincible; after all he had gotten sick in Florida when he was a contract laborer, but considering all that he had gone through and was able to achieve to this point in his new venture, this really shocked him. It was a major setback when he felt himself becoming ill. He became so sick that he couldn't get out of bed. He didn't have anyone to help him so he just remained in his room and tried to wait until he felt better to go out. Meanwhile, he was not reporting to work, and hadn't paid his rent which was due. After 3 days Ms. Roberts came to knock on Orthnell's door and find out what was going on. When she knocked, he mustered the strength and came to the door. When he opened he saw her standing there. "I haven't seen you in a couple of days" she said. "Ms. Roberts, I am so sick." Orthnell replied. Ms. Roberts was understanding and didn't make a big deal about the rent. She did have some bad news for him though. The Park Lane had sent him a telegram telling him that he was fired for not reporting to work. She also told him to go to the health clinic on Lexington Avenue to be seen by a doctor. He followed her advice and went.

After making his way to the health clinic, he found out that he had contracted the flu apparently for the second time. He was given a shot of some sort and sent home with orders to remain in bed. He stayed in bed for a couple more days until he felt strong enough to go out. This time around though, he had a tougher time finding work. He went to several locations inquiring about jobs. He went to the Apollo Theater which was only a couple of blocks from the boarding house where he lived, and various restaurants both in Harlem and downtown, but nothing stuck right away.

While he waited for responses to his inquiries about employment Orthnell began to orient himself with the various forms of entertainment that Harlem had to offer. He still had some money left from his days working in Florida. During the days Orthnell made it a custom to take in a couple of movies. He grew to enjoy cowboy movies starring actors such as Roy Rogers, Lash Larue, and Jeff Chandler. He also saw Johnny Weismuler as Tarzan for the first time. At night he took in shows at the Apollo where he saw the likes of James Brown, Frankie Lyman, and Little Anthony and the Imperials. Needless to say, Harlem was really starting to grow on Orthnell. He was enjoying his life there and starting to appreciate all that the city and America had to offer.

After returning from the movies one day, Ms. Roberts gave Orthnell a message that a restaurant in need of a waiter called and asked for him. It turns out that the restaurant was a gourmet place on the 15th floor of the Empire State building. He immediately hopped on a bus and went there. He had already purchased black pants, a bright white shirt, and a black bow tie as he knew that most of the workers in fancier restaurants dressed this way. The only thing he needed was a black vest, which they gave him. He started work right away. Finding this job was quite a relief as he would now be able to easily pay his rent and keep up with his life of entertainment at night and on his off days.

Things were looking up for Orthnell. He was quickly growing into adulthood in what he thought was the greatest city on earth. He turned 17 in June of 1956. He didn't really have friends yet and didn't have much to mark an event like his birthday, but he was content and optimistic. He was working and had a place to live, which meant more than just about anything else at this point.

The one thing that he had not managed to do yet was go to the Savoy Ballroom. Orthnell desperately wanted to go to the Savoy, one of the most happening places for Blacks in all of New York. Located between 140th and 141st on Lenox Avenue, this was the premier music and dance hall for Blacks in Harlem. It was there that the area's finest men and women got dressed up in their best clothes and came to dance the latest dances and socialize. Orthnell wanted his chance to go to the Savoy and that is what he did one Friday night after he got off work. He quickly hopped a bus uptown to change into the clothes he had purchased just for the occasion and walked to the Savoy. As he walked, he thought about what it would be like inside the Savoy. He especially anticipated the beautiful women he would see. As he approached the door, he could partially see the happenings inside: men in fine suits, women with shimmering dresses, and the sound of great music, laughter, and conversation. He walked up to the man guarding the door, reached in his pocket to pull out his admission fee and tried to hand it to the gentleman and to his chagrin he was politely rebuffed. "Sorry little brother, you're too young." Immediately Orthnell's heart sank and a feeling of dejection he had never felt before almost overwhelmed him. Orthnell needed to be 21 to enter, and even though he was tall and mature for 17 he may have passed for 18 or maybe even 19, but 21 was a stretch. Without saying much, he simply turned and walked away. The walk back home was a sad one. He was all dressed up, had some money in his pocket, and nowhere to go. So, that night he simply relaxed in his room, eventually falling asleep, dreaming about the Savoy.

The next day, Saturday, Orthnell arose and went to work. He forgot about the Savoy for the time being. He continued to enjoy the movies and shows at the Apollo, but he was dead set on making it back to the Savoy. He decided that he would give it another shot. This time he would disguise himself to look older. He went and purchased a black fedora and sunshades to wear with his suit. He was already 6'3" so he was tall enough but just needed a couple of accessories to sell his more mature look. He waited a couple of weeks and made another attempt to get into the Savoy. To his delight there was a different man at the door and a long line. He made it there a little earlier this time. Maybe it was the time, the new guy, or his hat and shades. Whatever it was, he got in!

Once inside, Orthnell casually made his way around the place, patiently getting his bearings and strategizing how he would approach the dance floor which was no place for those without real moves. Orthnell was not intimidated though. He had grown up dancing, had been to several events at the Apollo and had some natural rhythm. As a tall, dark young man with a Caribbean accent he was fairly confident about the reception he would receive from any of the women he chose to approach for a dance. One of the first women he graced the dance floor with was a woman named Orita who lived in Brooklyn. Orthnell and Orita ended up dancing together most of the night. Once he was ready to leave, Orita who was much more acquainted with the fast life of New York City told Orthnell to come back tomorrow and that she looked forward to seeing him there. He too looked forward to seeing her. Orita represented the potential for a significant connection for Orthnell in a place that was still new to him and relatively uncharted. Needless to say, he was going to make every attempt to get back to the Savoy the next night.

The next day Orthnell woke up thinking about his night at the Savoy, his time dancing with Orita, and how he hoped that he would be able to get in again and do it all over. After work, he rushed home, showered, and put on his outfit from the night before. Once again, it worked, and he made it into the Savoy. And once again, Orita was there. Two nights in a row, in a great place with a beautiful woman who seemed to be interested in him. Things were looking up for Orthnell.

After their meetings at the Savoy, Orthnell began to visit Orita at her home in Brooklyn where she lived with her mother. Orthnell was also able to find a one-bedroom apartment in a building on 128th Street where he would only stay briefly. Between his visits to Brooklyn and her visiting him in Harlem, Orthnell and Orita developed a good friendship. As time went on, Orthnell began to share with Orita how he wanted to move out of the city and experience somewhere a little different, a little less crowded, and hectic. Orita could not promise him anything but she told him about her aunt, Josephine Wilkerson who lived in Peekskill, NY. Aunt Josephine had a house that she owned in a predominantly Black section of town. She lived there alone, so Orita thought she might be open to the idea of having a boarder for a while.

A few weeks went by, giving Orita time to discuss with her aunt the potential for Orthnell to come and stay with her. She seemed open to the idea, so Orthnell and Orita made the trip up in Orita's car, about one and a half hours to meet Aunt Josephine. Aunt Josephine was a nice woman that embraced Orthnell openly, welcoming him into her home. She was curious about his story and how he ended up in New York. Orthnell simply told her that he had come there to find work, leaving out the information about stowing away and being there illegally, of course. His charm, charisma, and compelling story were enough for Aunt Josephine to agree to allow Orthnell to stay there with her. Orthnell returned to Harlem for a couple of days to gather his things and cancel his lease on his apartment. Orita picked him up again and drove him to Peekskill.

The agreement between Orthnell and Aunt Josephine was for Orthnell to stay there rent free, find employment, and get firmly established in the States. In return for his board he agreed to help with various projects that Josephine needed done around the house, beginning with painting the whole interior of the house. Orthnell agreed to the arrangement, but never explained that he had never painted before and had no clue how to do such work. She even asked him "are you sure you can paint?" Orthnell was fearful that his inability to do certain tasks around the house might cause Josephine to change her mind so he replied emphatically, "Yes, Ms. Josephine!" And so began Orthnell's stent in Peekskill.

The first room he was to paint was the living room. The color that Josephine wanted was pink. So, she bought the paint, brushes, and rollers, and left Orthnell to his work. Now, even though Orthnell had never painted before he did know to move the furniture out of the way so that he could reach the walls, but he did not know that he needed to put drop cloths down to cover the floor. Once the first smatterings of paint hit the floor Orthnell went into a panic. He grabbed some rags and began to try and clean up the mess he had made. Initially all he did was make matters worse as he simply spread the paint around into a larger area. He then decided to go into the basement and look for some sort of cleaner. The only thing that looked remotely like a cleaner for this kind of task was a can of kerosene, so that's what he chose. Once back upstairs, he poured the kerosene onto the rags and tried again to get the paint and stains out. It worked well enough and he was able to get most of the spilled paint up without Josephine ever seeing the mess and knowing that her young Bahamian boarder was ignorant of the finer points of house painting. He had opened the windows and aired out the house enough that only a slight smell of kerosene remained in the air by the time she got home.

After his initial mistakes, Orthnell wised up and got newspapers which he spread about on the floors. He painted the entire house over the next several weeks. When he wasn't painting, he was out searching for work. He eventually found a job in a local diner waiting tables, which he did for about 3 months. He wasn't satisfied with his job at the diner though, and kept looking until he landed a job at the Peekskill Country Club, where he also waited tables. It paid more and was more of an upscale establishment. So, after a few months, Orthnell was fairly established in Peekskill and Aunt Josephine was happy with their arrangement. She even decided to teach Orthnell how to drive.

Once again Orthnell had found favor with someone that was able to help him on his journey. Now, Aunt Josephine wanted to teach Orthnell how to drive and how better to do that than to first start by helping him buy a car. Knowing that he was steadily employed, Josephine encouraged Orthnell to buy a car, which she would sign for on the condition that he would make the payments. One Saturday afternoon they went together to a used car dealer and purchased a used 1952 Ford Customline Coupe. Of course, he could not drive it home, but it wouldn't be long before he would be driving around Peekskill.

After they purchased the car, Josephine signed Orthnell up for driving lessons, of which he took about 4. Then, she decided to teach him herself, figuring that she was as good or better than a hired instructor and could save some money at the same time. After a while, he learned how to drive. She even taught him how to make the appropriate hand signals for turning and how to drive in the snow which would be essential in New York. Aunt Josephine grew quite fond of Orthnell and considered it her duty to help him get established in a life in the U.S., help that would prove to be invaluable as time went on. She even started referring to him affectionately as "Al" which was short for Alfredo, his middle name. He hated this nickname, but he loved Aunt Josephine, so it was ok.

Everything was not all roses in Peekskill. Orthnell was working at the Country Club, was driving now, and had a stable place to live, but the social scene in Peekskill proved to be a little challenging to navigate for young Orthnell. He turned 18 in Peekskill and celebrated his birthday quietly with Aunt Josephine. She made him a small cake that they ate together in her kitchen. It wasn't like being home, but Aunt Josephine was all the family he had at the time and that was enough.

He began to drive to and from work, and on the weekends, he would go to a club called the Melody Inn. It was the place in Peekskill where many young Blacks could dance, eat, and socialize, much like the places in Harlem where Orthnell went, but not as large, or as glamorous. One night at the Melody Inn Orthnell had a run-in with one of the local men. He was older than Orthnell and slightly bigger, and was clearly agitated. "I heard you been messing with my girl!" the man yelled as he walked toward Orthnell. At this point Orthnell was clueless because he didn't know who the man was talking about. It may be that he danced with her or had a passing conversation with her, but before he could respond, the man sucker punched him in the face knocking him to the ground. Orthnell, being agile, immediately jumped to his feet and upper cut the man. Then, an all-out fight ensued until it was broken up by some other men in the club.

Orthnell stood his ground, but after the fight he left the Melody Inn intent on retrieving a pistol he had purchased in Harlem. As he drove home, his fury almost got the best of him as he considered the fact that he had no idea why he was accosted and the audacity the man displayed in swinging on him. By the time he reached Aunt Josephine's house he had calmed down and reconsidered going back to "handle" the man who so violated him. In many ways he had a lot to lose. He had stowed away and made it to Florida, then to New York, had seen some of the greatest soul artists at the Apollo, danced at the Savoy, met Orita, then Aunt Josephine, had stable work, and even had a car. To go back to the Melody Inn and possibly kill the man who he had never seen before or knew his name would have forfeited everything that he had achieved thus far. Instead, he stayed home and went to sleep. In fact, he never went to the Melody Inn again.

Perhaps it was the incident at the Melody Inn, or maybe the fact of his undocumented status, or some combination of factors, but after about 6 months in Peekskill with Aunt Josephine, Orthnell decided that it was time to go home. His goal was to make it to New York. That being achieved, he began planning his trip home. He had been in the U.S. for about 3 years and had had no family nearby to support him, and was living under the radar as an undocumented person. It makes sense that he may have just missed home and maybe even felt depressed about his situation. I make these inferences in part because not long before he decided to return to the Bahamas, he moved out of Aunt Josephine's house and moved into his own apartment in Peekskill, an indication that he was planning on staying. Whatever the case was, he decided to turn himself in to immigration authorities and begin the process of returning to the Bahamas.

In order to leave he would have to fly. There would be no stowing away to go back to the Bahamas as he had done to get out. For this, Orthnell knew he would have to report himself to U.S. immigration authorities and get official status and approval to leave the country. One morning on his off day he took a bus to Manhattan to the Federal Immigration building. When he went in he waited to speak to an immigration officer and explained his situation. At first the officer was amazed to hear his story and to know that Orthnell had been in the country for so long without detection or any significant problems. He then told Orthnell that it would be about one month before he would be granted the documentation necessary to purchase his plane ticket and leave the country. This would provide Orthnell enough time to get things in order; things like cancelling his lease, letting his boss at the Country Club know that he was leaving, and figuring out what to do with his car.

He decided to give his car to Aunt Josephine; he never found out what she did with it. She and Orthnell would part ways on very good terms. Orthnell was always well mannered; anything he was asked to do, like paint the house, he did gladly, and even though she never wanted him to, he gave her money periodically to help with household expenses. Aunt Josephine was disappointed when he left, but just as he had found his own job and eventually his own apartment, she was there just to help him get along with his life, which she did very nobly.

Once Orthnell went back to the immigration office and got the necessary documents, it was time to catch a bus back to Florida in order to catch a plane home. He would travel one more time to Ft. Lauderdale where he purchased a ticket for a Mackey Airlines flight. Mackey International was one of the main air travel providers between Florida and the Bahamas from the late 40s until the late 60s when it was bought by Eastern Airlines (Eastern). Then, Eastern went out of business in 1991 (History).

HOME AGAIN

His flight lasted less than an hour and before he knew it he was landing in Nassau after having left when he was fifteen. Immediately when the plane landed Orthnell reported to the immigration office. He approached an immigration official, a White man, who asked him where he had been. "I've been in America." "What?" "You're lying." "How'd you get there?" "I stowed away." The man didn't believe Orthnell at first, but once he showed him his paperwork from the States his story began to seem more believable. Orthnell was a man now. He was 18, soon to be 19 and was not in the mood for hiding his story or his intentions anymore. He had achieved his goal of not only making it to the U.S., but to New York City, had some success and proved that he could survive there. The immigration official soon realized that he had someone before him who had done something inconceivable to many, and he quickly granted him passage into his home country with simply a shake of his head and a few rubber stamps.

The first place that Orthnell went was to his cousin Charlotte's house. Charlotte was Uncle Lar's daughter and someone Orthnell was close to. Once he arrived at Charlotte's he found out that Joshua had moved. He wasn't far away, but it was a new location none the less and news to Orthnell. He tried to explain to Charlotte and his other relatives that lived with her where he had been and how he got there. They didn't quite get the idea of him stowing away or simply didn't believe him. It all was somewhat puzzling to them; so much so that eventually Orthnell just dropped the subject and went to find his father.

Joshua had moved from Wesley Corner to Dumping Ground Corner, a few streets away. When he got there Joshua greeted him with a typical, "boy, where you been?" "I've been in America." At this Joshua did something that Orthnell was not accustomed to seeing from his very stern, stoic father; he laughed. In Orthnell's mind he thought that his father didn't think he was smart enough to make it to America, let alone survive there for the length of time that he did. Orthnell didn't spend too much time trying to convince his father of what he had accomplished. He simply asked him for a place where he could sleep for a while until he decided his next move.

Orthnell ended up staying with Joshua for about 3 months, further extending the time that he had not seen his mother. He had not seen Rose since he was 15. It is difficult to comprehend this type of separation from the person who gave birth to him, loved him only as a mother could, and raised him, yet Orthnell believed it was essential to making him the man he was to become. Even so, after 3 months in Nassau with Joshua he decided to make the trip to Andros to see Rose and his other family members.

He would catch a flight on a small propeller plane home. When he arrived at the small airport in Andros, something that was not there when he left, he asked a man that he saw if he knew Henderson. To his surprise the man replied "there's Henderson over there." Henderson had begun driving a cab, primarily taking travelers from the airport to their desired destinations throughout Andros, something that worked out well for Orthnell. It took a few long seconds for it to register with Henderson that he was looking at his younger brother, taller now and bearing the confidence of a man of experiences and achievement. "Where you been?" "Mother already wear the burying shroud for you." "She thought you were dead." These were Henderson's first remarks when he saw his long-lost brother. "Well, I'm alive; I'm ok," Orthnell replied. Henderson hugged and kissed his brother on the cheek, signs that he was glad to see him and that he was alive. They stood for a few moments smiling at each other. "You gone give me a ride?" Orthnell asked. "Sure. Come on." Orthnell put his bag in the back seat and got in.

On the ride to see Rose Orthnell was hesitant to offer much information about his adventures in America and the details of his departure from home and the lives of those who loved him. Even though Henderson was happy to see his younger brother Orthnell knew that there could be some sore feelings. He knew that Henderson definitely would have some things to say about him leaving the way that he did and the emotional distress and hardship he caused Rose, his grandmother Alma who died about a year after he left, and others. So, using wisdom, Orthnell remained quiet for most of the ride. To his surprise Henderson didn't say much either and didn't launch into any disciplinary rants that he had experienced as a youngster.

When they arrived at Rose's house Orthnell got his bag and walked up to the front door. Rose had already heard the car pull up and immediately opened the door, not knowing that it was her son whom she had already mourned for when she thought he was surely dead. Amazement and elation immediately filled Rose as tears began to roll down her face and she shouted "Thank you Jesus, Thank you Jesus!" She grabbed Orthnell and hugged him with a grip that suggested that she had resolved to never see him again and she never wanted him out of her sight. "You don't know how many sleepless nights I had over you" Rose proceeded to tell him. Orthnell simply listened and smiled, telling her "I'm alright mother, I'm alright." It would take some time for her to adjust to the reality that her "boy" had come home. But, she would do it and the relationship between Rose and Orthnell would slowly be restored. As word spread that Orthnell had returned, many people, his friends, aunts, uncles and cousins came to see him and welcome him home.

Rose planned a celebration for Orthnell at the Society Hall in Andros, the same place where Christmas and other celebrations were held. People from all over the community, friends and family came to rejoice at Orthnell's return. Musicians of all sorts came to the hall playing calypso music. There were those playing wind instruments and drums. Then there were those playing the saw board and the washboard. The saw board was literally a makeshift instrument where a man would drag a saw along a piece of wood, producing a rhythmic, sawing sound. The combination made for a great, festive time. People danced, sang, and ate for hours, well into the night. Orthnell realized at this moment how much he was loved by his family and his community. He was appreciative and even felt some remorse for some of the pain he had caused some of his family and friends, especially Rose, but he did not dwell in that emotional place. He continued to enjoy the music and dancing and the great Bahamian dishes he missed while he was in the States.

Orthnell remained in Andros for only 2 months. While he was there he re-acclimated himself with the home of his boyhood. He reconnected with his friends and family members that were glad to see him. He even had time to spend with a couple of young women: Miriam Cantor and Sally Rolle. Of course, neither acquaintance became too serious as Orthnell knew he would be leaving again soon. And, after the somewhat fast life of New York and his trysts with a multitude of women before that, the women and life in general in Andros had lost much of any appeal that it had held for Orthnell. When this was all that he knew it was fine, but Orthnell had a taste of a much vaster world beyond the humble Andros.

In the years that he was gone Orthnell noticed some changes on the island. One of the biggest was that the sawmill had grown and was employing more of the local men. Many of those who were once dedicated fishermen were now making their livings in the mill. As a result of the mill, there were more motor vehicles throughout Andros, namely trucks. In the mills men were learning the art of lumbering, how to cut and finish wood for sale. There was also a large, new food store on the island. More than likely this was something that was also influenced by the mill as more people had money to spend and more people were commuting to Andros to work. This all most likely precipitated the building of the Andros airport as well.

As for Orthnell, he spent much of his time at home fishing. He had a crew of friends that he had known from boyhood that he was getting reestablished with: Edgar, Junior, Joseph, Solomon, Joe, and Sidney. Together, Orthnell and his 6 friends would hang out and fish together. The young men did this on a daily basis and it was something that Orthnell missed while he was gone. Eventually, when he would return to the States for good, he tried to fish the U.S. way with spinning tackle, and never liked it. At home, Orthnell fished with a staff, basically a two-pronged spear used to spear fish that came into view using his water-glass. If they did not use the spear they simply used a string and a hook, baited usually with crab meat to lure the fish and then hook them if they attempted to bite the bait. Traditional activities like this and the camaraderie that he was enjoying with his friends were important to Orthnell. He had not known these familiar activities, sites, and friends for several years and they were welcome signs that he was home.

THE TOWERS

After about 2 months in Andros Orthnell was getting the itch to leave again. So, he packed up what things he had and began the process of telling Rose and others goodbye. He was planning to go back to Nassau to find work, which he did. He would again stay with Joshua and his family, who welcomed him back. The job that Orthnell landed was as the captain of a small sightseeing boat that took tourists from Nassau to Paradise Island. Paradise Island was and is a popular destination off the coast of Nassau that is replete with beautiful beaches, wildlife, and resorts. The boat, *Lady Paradise* chartered as many as 10 vacationers 25 to 30 minutes from Nassau to Paradise Island allowing them to look through its glass bottom at the sea life and coral beneath.

As with many things that simply seemed to go Orthnell's way he happened upon this job by being in the right place at the right time. The owner of the *Lady Paradise*, Clarence Colbrooke needed a captain as his usual captain did not show up on the day when he approached Orthnell. As was his custom, Orthnell went to the docks and spent time there when he was in need of work. As he had done to so many before, he impressed Mr. Colbrooke with his comportment and stature. It didn't take long for Orthnell to accept the job when it was offered to him. The *Lady Paradise* was propelled by an inboard gasoline engine. All that Orthnell had to do was use

the steering wheel and keep the boat on course and steady so that his passengers arrived on the island contented and ready to soak up the sites and
spend money at the many attractions there.

On one of his first trips Orthnell met a young White couple, Mr. and Mrs.
Towers. The husband William B. Towers, a lawyer, and his wife Jane were va-
cationing in the Bahamas while their young family was being cared for back at
their home in Jacksonville, FL. The Towers were in their early thirties and excited to experience all that the Bahamas had to offer. On this fateful day they
were fortunate to have Orthnell as their captain. Charming and engaging,
Orthnell shared with them the history and culture of the island as they cruised.
He also described for them the rich aquatic life beneath them as they jour-
neyed; all things he learned during his years growing up and spending much
time on and in the water. Occasionally he would pay each of them a compli-
ment and kept them contented with humor and pleasantries. Once they arrived
at Paradise Island the Towers got off and spent the usual 4 hours experiencing
the island and Orthnell waited to take them back to Nassau.

The Towers, like most people had a great time on Paradise Island and
were quite happy when they returned to the *Lady Paradise* and Orthnell. On
the trip back to Nassau Mr. Towers initiated an interesting and almost unbelievable conversation with Orthnell. He told Orthnell that he wanted him to
return to Florida and be their butler and chauffer. The tall, dark, charming
19-year-old had been more impressive than he even knew, and little did he
know that this trip aboard the *Lady Paradise* was going to change the course of
his life forever. But, initially Orthnell was in disbelief with what Bill Towers
was telling him. This disbelief was not the kind of disbelief that stemmed from
a person's overwhelming excitement brought on by deep aspirations meeting
a spectacular opportunity. It stemmed from his general distrust of Whites and
a belief in their fickleness and disingenuous dealings with people of color. "I
know how you people are," he responded with a smile when Bill Towers told
him how much he and his wife liked him. "No, we're serious," Mr. Towers responded, and Jane affirmed his assertion. Apparently they had talked about
Orthnell and the possibility of him coming to work for them while they were
on Paradise Island. "Come to our Hotel when we return to Nassau and we'll
show you," Mr. Towers told him and that is just what Orthnell did.

Once they got back to Nassau, Orthnell walked with the Towers back to
their hotel. Once there, Mr. and Mrs. Towers went to their room while Orthnell

waited in the lobby. They returned with $500.00 and gave it to him telling him to use it to get ready to come and visit them in Jacksonville. This "deposit" proved at least 2 things to Orthnell. One was that they were at least partially serious about their proposition. The other was that they were people of substantial means. As far as he knew, no one he had ever met was able to so readily dispose of $500.00 and this without any guarantee that they would get any return on their investment. Though he was impressed with the money Orthnell's response was lukewarm at best. He did tell them that he would consider visiting them in Jacksonville, but to completely get on board with such a plan with people he had only met that day was something that no reasonable person would do. He took the money though, and his principles would ultimately dictate his actions from that point on.

When he left the Towers' hotel he went home. Once there he told Joshua and Lolitta about what had happened and that he was considering doing it. From Joshua Orthnell received an expected less than enthusiastic response and no litany of questions or cautionary words that a parent might offer in a situation like this. Lolitta was different though. She was excited and assured Orthnell that this was a fortunate occurrence and that she would help him prepare, which she did.

Orthnell continued working on the *Lady Paradise* while he prepared to leave. The Towers had told him that they would send him a round trip airline ticket which they did about six weeks later. Again he would fly Mackie Airlines, and over the six weeks he had grown excited to go and see where the Towers lived and what kind of life they had to offer him in Jacksonville. Lolitta had helped him by ironing his clothes and making sure that he had all of the essential items that he might need. Before leaving he made a brief trip to Andros to say goodbye to Rose. Once again, Rose would be grappling with her son leaving the islands. It wasn't as though she wasn't accustomed to months, even years apart from him, and at least this time she would have advanced notice and know where he was. None of this made the news of his plans any easier for her. When he gave her the news she cautioned him about trusting Whites. Having grown up in a place that was almost exclusively Black, the idea of trusting strange Whites from America was not something anyone in their situation would readily embrace, but Rose wanted to support her son. It is easy to understand that Rose saw her son trying to make a good future for himself, and she had to have sensed that

Orthnell's future was not going to be limited to the Bahamas and definitely not to Andros.

Orthnell left on July 20, 1959, not long after celebrating his 20th birthday. After bidding his family and friends goodbye, he headed to the Andros airport to catch a Mackey flight that was due to arrive in Ft. Lauderdale at 2:00 PM. After landing in Ft. Lauderdale he would then have to take a bus to Jacksonville. Once he arrived at the airport, he retrieved his bags and took a taxi to the Greyhound Bus Station. By the time he reached the bus station it was about 5:00. He would have to wait several more hours for the next bus that would leave for Jacksonville at about 11:00 PM.

While waiting in the bus station Orthnell had an encounter with a couple of men attempting to get some money off of him. They were two Black men and they approached Orthnell casually and asked him "where do you keep your money, brother?" "It's in my suitcase," Orthnell responded. This was not true however, but Orthnell knew that had he told the two men the truth that every cent that he had was on his person they would have without a doubt robbed him. In fact, his suitcase had already been checked in and would soon be loaded onto the next bus to Jacksonville. For some reason the men believed him and simply walked away. Orthnell didn't know where the men went, but he was relieved to know that he had averted what could have been a very bad situation. It also served as an ominous warning about some of the people he would need to be leery of in Florida. Sadly, those people looked like him, not the Whites that he had been warned about.

The bus drove all night to Jacksonville, slowly along U.S. Route 1, making dozens of stops along the way to let passengers off and pick up new ones. They finally arrived at about 9:00 in the morning. Needless to say Orthnell was tired and hungry when he arrived. Mr. Towers knew that he would be in an important meeting when Orthnell arrived, so he sent one of his friends, a lawyer like him, to pick Orthnell up. The friend's name was Mr. Rye. Mr. Rye was not quite as busy as he was on that morning, so he was happy to help out his friend. The Towers had informed Orthnell that Mr. Rye would pick him up so it was no surprise. The 20-minute ride from the bus station to the Towers' home was a quiet one. Even though Orthnell knew that Mr. Rye was picking him up, he didn't know him. It is understandable that he wouldn't have much to say.

Mr. Rye arrived with Orthnell around 10:00. Mrs. Towers, the 4 Towers children: Betsy (13), Billy (11), John (9), and Agnes (5), and Helen Green, the

Towers' maid, were there to greet him. Mrs. Towers and the children came out to welcome Orthnell, and they did so warmly. The children were especially excited to meet Orthnell. It would become very important for Orthnell to get along well with the Towers children. He would be transporting them to and from school once it started back up in the fall and they would be a constant presence day to day in the Towers' home as Orthnell went about doing his work. Mrs. Towers gave Orthnell a big, warm hug and asked about his trip. "It was long, but good," he told her. He didn't mention the conmen or anything else that would cast a negative light on his experience. He was able to sleep on the long bus ride from Ft. Lauderdale, so he was not completely exhausted, but he never even brought up the need for rest or anything like that.

Once everyone greeted each other, Mrs. Towers walked Orthnell inside to show him their home. As their wealth and generosity exhibited on their island vacation suggested, the Towers had a beautiful, ranch-style home, spacious, and attended by their full-time maid, and soon young Orthnell. After showing him around the house which Orthnell actually believed was modest considering their wealth. As they toured the house Mrs. Towers described for Orthnell what his responsibilities would be. As stated before, Orthnell would be responsible for getting the Towers children to and from school safely. His primary job on a daily basis though would be attending to Mr. Towers. He would be his valet. Each day Orthnell would prepare Mr. Towers' clothes for work and drive him to work once he had dropped off the children at school. He would also be an assistant to Helen in the kitchen and in serving meals. There would be times when Orthnell would be called on to do other jobs as well that were not necessarily in his "job description" such as raking leaves in the fall and cleaning up after the children when needed. He would be on duty officially from Monday to Friday. His work hours were from 7:30 in the morning until the evening when the children had eaten dinner and Mr. Towers was squared away after work, having eaten and retired for the evening, which sometimes was after nightfall. In reality there were no set times for his on-duty hours; he was always on call, except on the weekends when he was officially off.

Mrs. Towers took Orthnell to show him where he would be sleeping. The Towers had a living space adjacent to their 2-car garage. It was a comfortable dwelling. In fact, it was more spacious and comfortable than other places he had come to call home. As a youth, Orthnell was accustomed to sleeping on the floor, sometimes in cramped quarters with several family members. He had a tiny space to sleep at the monastery. He slept in barracks with groups of other men on the farms in Florida. At his friend Percy Marshall's he was sharing a space on a borrowed bed or couch. So, needless to say, having a bed of his own and some space to store his things and move around was quite agreeable to him. Hanging in his place was his "uniform" which consisted of a black tuxedo, fully equipped with a starched shirt and black bow tie. There was also a chauffer's cap that he was to wear when he was driving. Orthnell was impressed with the clothes and was anxious to try them on and get started with his work which would commence the very next day. Orthnell's "visit" became the offiicial introductioin to his job. He decided to stay and work for the Towers.

After showing Orthnell where he would be staying they went back into the house where he formally met the Towers' maid, Helen. Helen was a nice woman and warm toward Orthnell. She knew that he was young and in a strange place, so she made every effort to welcome him and make him feel comfortable. She was an African-American woman in her mid-50s and she knew a great deal about the challenges of being Black in the South, dealing with segregation, working for Whites in their homes, and also the benefits of having a family like the Towers who as Orthnell would learn were fair and caring people. Needless to say Orthnell had a great deal to learn from "Aunt Helen" as he would soon begin to call her. Getting to know her and eventually her husband Ned was vital to Orthnell adjusting to his new life with the Towers. Orthnell would grow very close to Aunt Helen, eventually going to stay some weekends with her and Ned so that he could experience the Black community of Jacksonville.

Helen had dinner ready at about 5:00 that evening as she always did. She was a good cook and had worked for the Towers for several years, and this would be Orthnell's first sampling of her southern cuisine. Orthnell was expected to learn some of Helen's cooking techniques and assist her in the kitchen, eventually taking over some of the cooking responsibilities if Helen had her hands full with cleaning the Towers home or doing laundry, etc. This would help him later in life, serving as another training ground in the culinary arts. Dinner was served for Mrs. Towers and the children first and then Helen prepared a plate for Orthnell which he ate alone in the kitchen. One might think that on his first night in the Towers' home that he would have eaten with them, but that was not the case. He simply ate the plate of food Helen had prepared for him and went back to his place to rest. Actually, the Towers did not sit down together regularly to eat dinner. Being that one of his primary roles was to look after the Towers children, Orthnell would sit them down at the dining table for their meals, including dinner. Mrs. Towers would sit down with them sometimes, but not always, and Mr. Towers usually came home long after dinnertime.

Not only was he a busy, dedicated lawyer, Mr. Towers also enjoyed having drinks after work. At times Orthnell would be called upon to go and pick a more than tipsy Mr. Towers up after he stopped to have a few drinks after work. Orthnell never saw Mr. Towers violent or ever using his indulgence in alcohol as an excuse to neglect or abuse his family, but it did at times keep him away from them longer than he otherwise would be. Mr. Towers finally arrived at home at about 8:30. As soon as he did, he went out to speak with Orthnell. Orthnell heard a knock at his door and when he opened he was pleased to see Mr. Towers, who greeted him with a wide-grinned smile and firm handshake. After asking Orthnell about his trip and making sure that he was situated well, he walked back into the house to eat and be with his family for the evening. After saying goodnight to Mr. Towers, Orthnell turned in for the night.

After parting with Mr. Towers Orthnell laid on his bed thinking about his life a bit. He wondered how he had arrived at such a place. He was 20 and in the home of a wealthy White family in America. Maybe it was destiny he thought. After all he had the desire to leave at such a young age and he was the only one of his immediate family to do so. He was tired and he knew he needed rest, but his mind continued to drift to thoughts of his youth, people back home, and what could possibly be awaiting him in the days, weeks, months, and years ahead. Finally, he drifted off to sleep.

THE FIRST DAY ON THE JOB

Orthnell rose on the first day of his life with the Towers with the sun. He was anxious to get his new adventure started, but he thought it was too early to go over to the house. He knew that Helen arrived at about 8:00, but that would be too late. Instead, he put on his tuxedo and waited until about 7:30 to make his way over to the house. When he did, he found only Mr. and Mrs. Towers awake. They were in the kitchen having coffee and toast. They welcomed him in, offered him something to eat and inquired about his rest and how he liked the accommodations. Of course, he told them that they were fine. Even if he had been miserable all night he wouldn't have told the Towers that. In fact, he truly found the place that they had prepared for him very much to his liking, and a comfortable place to call home for what would end up being three and a half years.

His first task on his first day on the job was to drive Mr. Towers to work. Mr. Towers worked in downtown Jacksonville which like the bus station was about 20 minutes from the Towers' home. The car that he drove was a brand new Lincoln Continental. It was not the only car that the Towers had, but it was the nicest. The other car was a Pontiac Safari Station Wagon which was used primarily when the whole family went together on an outing. The Lincoln was the nicest car that Orthnell had ever been in. In fact, the Lincoln Continental was one of the nicest cars that anyone could buy in America in those days. It had a smooth ride and handled well. Orthnell drove while Mr. Towers sat in the passenger seat giving him directions and pointing out landmarks and sites to help him remember how to get home. Whenever Orthnell drove Mr. Towers without any other family or people in the car he sat in the passenger seat instead of the back seat as one might think. Once Orthnell dropped Mr. Towers off he now had to make his way home which he did with minimal confusion. Mr. Towers had done a good job pointing out the things that Orthnell should look for on his way back.

Once back at the Towers' Orthnell spent the day primarily with Helen learning the ins and outs of the Towers' home. He helped her prepare lunch and dinner. He drove Mrs. Towers to a meeting with some of her friends at a nearby home. The children were left in the care of Helen. While Mrs. Towers was inside the home, Orthnell waited by the car until she was ready to leave. This was the typical scenario for the Towers' driver. If whoever Mr. or Mrs. Towers was meeting with also had hired domestics Orthnell would spend time socializing with them if they had time.

Some of the domestics that he grew relatively close to were the ones that worked for Mr. Towers' parents, Charlie and Elizabeth. Their domestics at the time were Charles and Emma. Charles was their butler and chauffer and Emma was their maid. Both were in their mid-50s and spent a great deal of time when they could talking to Orthnell and sharing their experiences with him, giving him advice, and generally being friendly and warm to him. Chef recalls many days chatting with Charles and Emma while the Towers visited. Just like Orthnell, who to this day does not have a negative word to utter about the Towers or a bad memory about them, Charles and Emma thought very highly of their employers and considered them fair and loving.

The elder Towers lived on an estate with a large home and some acres of land on the St. John River, a testament to their wealth acquired from years of having a successful legal practice which the Elder Mr. Towers passed down to his children. Bill, who Orthnell now worked for and lived with, Charles, Bill's brother, and their sister Betty were all lawyers in their family's firm. They were all doing very well in their practice and Orthnell stood to benefit greatly from the success of the Towers' law practice. After all, it was this success that brought him to Jacksonville in the first place. Bill and Jane visited Bill's parents often with their children. As a result, Orthnell got to know them and their domestics very well.

When they got back home, the Towers children were able to coax Orthnell into a game of hide and seek. This would be the first of many games that Orthnell would play with the Towers kids over the three and a half years that he would live with them. They would often play hide and seek, softball, and board games. These interactions with the Towers children served to solidify Orthnell's place in the Towers home and indeed in their family. Eventually Orthnell truly did begin to feel like a part of the Towers family.

Along with the children, Orthnell had to become acquainted with the family's two dogs, a black and white sheep dog and a brown boxer. Walking the dogs twice a day was another one of Orthnell's responsibilities, something he had to grow accustomed to. It wasn't so much the walking of the dogs per se. It was the general dislike he had for dogs. The only interactions he had with them previously were with the wild dogs in the Bahamas. The idea of living with dogs, or any animals for that matter was nothing that came easy for Orthnell. But, like most things on his life's journey so far he adjusted to it and learned to do what he needed to do in order to make it.

Something else he was introduced to on his first day was the family vegetable garden. Mrs. Towers intended for Orthnell to help tend it. He wouldn't be the exclusive gardener, but like many things around the Towers home, Orthnell was expected to avail himself when help was needed. This too, Orthnell grew to accept, but only for a while. The first gardening season passed and Orthnell helped when he was asked, but there was something about gardening or being used in this capacity that didn't sit well with him. As the next spring approached, after being with the Towers for almost a full year, and getting more comfortable with them, Orthnell informed them of his displeasure with the work. In his mind and partly what he expressed to them was that "I did not come here to be a gardener." He was perfectly fine with being a chauffeur and doing the work of a butler, playing with the kids, walking the dogs, but he did not want his hands down in the dirt, planting, pulling, or harvesting. Perhaps it evoked memories of his days on the Florida farms. They respected his wishes, and no longer asked or required him to work in the garden.

Orthnell was able to take a break in the middle of the day and rest. During this time he assessed what had transpired over the several hours in his official butler/chauffer capacity. Because it was the middle of summer he didn't have to drive the children to school so his job was a little more limited than it would be beginning in the fall. Instead, he focused most of his attention on Mr. Towers. As evening approached he prepared to drive back to Mr. Towers' office to pick him up. Once again, Mr. Towers would be coming home a bit later than the time when his family ate their dinner. Orthnell was able to eat and then he left to get Mr. Towers. On the way back Mr. Towers inquired about Orthnell's day and commented on his good driving abilities. Mr. Towers had no idea that Orthnell had lived in the States before and even owned a car when he was in New York. In fact, as far as the Towers ever knew, Orthnell had never been to the States. This was a bit of information that Orthnell never thought particularly important or relevant to share with them. This fits perfectly into Orthnell's desire to not "be found out" even though he was no longer an illegal immigrant. For whatever reason he thought it was to his advantage to have the Towers believe that it was their act of choosing him to come to work for them that brought him to the land of opportunity. Mr. Towers had a skilled, dedicated driver and that was all that mattered really.

Because Mr. Towers often kept hours that didn't exactly coincide with his family's he and Orthnell grew particularly close. Whenever Orthnell had to pick Mr. Towers up particularly late he would do so, bring Mr. Towers home, and prepare his food. If Mr. Towers didn't care to eat what Helen had made he would ask Orthnell to prepare a dish that he called "dupee." Sometimes after a long day, capped off with a few drinks, he would say to Orthnell, "son, fix me some of that Dupee." What he was referring to was a dish of corned beef and rice. Orthnell was never sure why Mr. Towers enjoyed it so much, but whenever he requested it he got it. After eating, Mr. Towers retired for the evening. His clothes for the next day had already been prepared by Orthnell, so his evening and late night belonged to himself, and Orthnell would be there to meet him in the morning to assist him in his preparation for the day.

Aside from driving Mr. Towers Orthnell also would drive friends and clients of Mr. Towers when the need arose. This required Orthnell to maintain an immaculate appearance. He was always clean shaven, clothes pressed, and hair well-kempt. Orthnell was a tall, 20-year-old articulate man, with a distinguished Bahamian accent. This made his presentation exceptional and the Towers were proud to have others see him. He grew very conscious of the need to represent himself and the Towers well in whatever circles they navigated.

THE GREENS

Orthnell had a positive time for the duration of his years with the Towers. One of the special aspects of his experience was the relationship that he developed with Aunt Helen. Helen took on somewhat of a motherly role for Orthnell. She intentionally tried to teach him vital life lessons. Just like the Towers, Helen did not know about Orthnell's experiences in Florida and New York before he met the Towers, so she felt that there was much for Orthnell to learn about life in America, especially in the South. It was 1959 and race relations in the country were, well, what they were in 1959; in need of improvement to say the least. Orthnell was just happy to have the attention. At 20 years old he had spent a considerable portion of his life away from his own mother and other loving relatives, so to have Helen take an interest in him was more than welcomed by Orthnell and a great comfort to him.

The interest in Orthnell led Helen to eventually invite Orthnell to come and stay with her and her husband Ned one weekend a month, while he was off. As stated before Orthnell's official schedule was Monday through Friday. His weekends were for himself. Helen and Ned lived about a half hour from the Towers home by bus, and Orthnell would leave on Friday evening, once all that he needed to do was taken care of.

Helen and Ned lived in an all-Black section of the city called Moncrief. Orthnell was extremely excited to go there on the weekends. When he was with the Towers he did not see Blacks, save for those, who like him worked for Whites. On a day-to-day basis he did not see or socialize with ordinary Black citizens whom he could establish relationships with, something that would be vital for any person in his situation. While staying with the Greens Orthnell was able to check out the Black social scene. He would go to night-clubs often and generally enjoyed himself as any 20-year-old would. Helen even introduced Orthnell to eligible young women who were "worth his time" in Helen's mind. One such woman was Mae, a 30-year-old schoolteacher. Mae lived on the same street as Helen, was single, and very attractive. She had a light complexion, a medium frame, and was fun to be around. Orthnell would even stay the night with Mae from time to time.

As time went on and Orthnell went to stay with Helen and Ned he was introduced to more and more people, establishing those friendships and connections that would solidify his sense of belonging in Jacksonville. Eventually Orthnell would meet more women as well and began to want to have more of a friendship with Mae than anything extremely serious or permanent. Mae was not happy with the idea of a friendship with Orthnell. After all she had been nice to him, showed him around Jacksonville, and did all that indicated her romantic desires. Mae was a professional woman with a car, so she had provided him the means to get around the city and go to the spots where the Black population spent their time. Nevertheless, she had no choice but to let any thoughts of a long-term commitment sub-side. Orthnell was young, handsome, and had money enough to treat any young woman well. He wasn't going to settle for a serious commitment at this point in his life.

There were also male friends that Orthnell looked forward to spending time with when he went to stay with Helen and Ned as well. One of these friends, Earl Geiger, was just the type of guy that young Orthnell wanted to be around. Earl was an older, bigger guy, extremely strong and had no fear of anyone. He drove a Harley Davidson motorcycle and was extremely popular in Moncrief. Whenever Orthnell was with Earl, Orthnell didn't have to worry about any problems that might arise. Earl was adept at handling himself and commanded a great amount of respect. He and Orthnell would ride around Jacksonville, hanging out, meeting women, and having a great time. Over time Orthnell began calling Earl almost as soon as he arrived at the Green's. Earl would come by on his Harley and the fun would begin.

Getting picked up by Earl was cool, but eventually Orthnell would want his own wheels to get around with. The Towers had graciously allowed Orthnell to borrow their Pontiac station wagon to go back and forth to the Green's once a month or so, and wherever else he may have wanted to go on the weekends or evenings, but eventually Orthnell wanted some transportation of his own. Having saved up a few hundred dollars he decided to purchase a moped. It was a late 50s model, red, and not very fast. Orthnell tolerated his ride for several months, but eventually spoke with Mr. Towers about needing something faster. Upon hearing this, Mr. Towers decided to shop for and buy Orthnell his own motorcycle. It was a slightly used Honda. Mr. Towers paid about $700.00 for the bike and Orthnell was ecstatic. This not only helped Orthnell's status in the communities where he spent his free time, it also helped to solidify the relationship between he and the Towers, Mr. Towers especially. Not long after starting to work for the Towers they had helped him open his first bank account with the money that they had paid him with. Now, they did something similar to an act of a parent towards a loved or deserving son.

MIDDLEBURG

Over time, as Orthnell met more and more people, he became acquainted with a few from Middleburg, about 30 miles south of Jacksonville. Middleburg would prove to be a significant place in Orthnell's life as he would meet his first wife Lena there. Lena Mae Mack was about Orthnell's age, very pretty, with a brown complexion, and had a strict mother, Ms. Missy Mack, who would not sit idly by and allow her only daughter to be wooed helplessly by a strapping young islander like Orthnell. Ms. Missy raised Lena in a religious household where church attendance was mandatory and having a "night life" was not accepted. Needless to say Ms. Missy was on her guard when Lena began speaking about Orthnell and wanting to spend time with him. Lena and Orthnell were introduced by a mutual friend, and almost instantly had an attraction to each other. For Orthnell, relating to women had always been easy, and he had access to plenty in the Jacksonville area, but Lena was different. Lena was not into the social scene like most of the women Orthnell knew in Jacksonville; she came from a religious, strict home, and by no means would she be an easy conquest. She had no apparent vices and was very intelligent, a person Orthnell needed in his life and was worth getting very serious about.

So, the courtship began. On the weekends, Orthnell would drive his motorcycle to Lena's house, where they would sit talking with Ms. Missy close by. Occasionally she would give Orthnell permission to take Lena out for a ride. When she did, they would often go to the park or to the beach to enjoy nature and talk. They didn't go clubbing or dancing, as was customary for Orthnell, but focused mostly on conversation and learning about each other through focused time alone or under the watchful eye of Ms. Missy.

It wasn't long before Orthnell asked Lena to marry him, and in June, 1961 they married, after about a year of courtship. They were both 22. The wedding took place in a small Baptist Church in Middleburg and was attended by about 75 guests. The Towers did not attend, though they were very supportive and encouraging, something that will be made extremely clear shortly. Their lack of attendance was most likely a reflection of the racial climate and norms. De facto Segregation was still very much the rule of the day, and neither Orthnell nor the Towers made overt steps to violate that rule. They honeymooned for 2 weeks in Daytona Beach at the house of one of Lena's brothers, Horace and his wife Yvonne. The Towers were more than happy to give Orthnell the time off to honeymoon with his new bride. Even more significant than the time off was the two bedroom house that Mr. Towers had built for Orthnell and Lena in Middleburg not long before their wedding. Orthnell had purchased a 100 x 100 ft. piece of land on which the wooden structure would be built. Mr. Towers furnished the down payment and had the mortgage in his name. The payments however, would be Orthnell's responsibility. Once they returned from Daytona Beach to their new home, Orthnell resumed his duties at the Towers, commuting every day from Middleburg to Jacksonville.

In March, 1962, when he was 23, his first child, a son, was born. He and Lena decided to name him Orthnell. Orthnell was elated at the birth of his son. He was now a true family man. By the end of 1962 Orthnell was also ready to seek out an identity and life for himself and his family apart from the Towers. He had reached the conclusion that it was time to leave the people that brought him to the U.S. permanently, gave him a financial foundation, bought him transportation, and even built him his first home. Orthnell would eventually relinquish the house and land over to Mr. Towers. In the meantime he kept living there with his young family and continued making the mortgage payments. Orthnell was and is eternally grateful for what the Towers had done for him, but there was more that Orthnell wanted from life than being a wealthy White family's butler. The relationship between the Towers and Orthnell would not be severed by his departure and that relationship continues to this day with the Towers children. Mr. and Mrs. Towers have both passed away.

Late in 1962 Orthnell left Middleburg, going 145 miles south to Titusville, near the coast, where his friend Jeremiah Pritchett was able to help him get a job at a soap factory. Lena and little Orthnell would stay in Middleburg. Not only did Orthnell go, but he took several young men from Middleburg who were in need of work with him. Having money saved up from his years of working with the Towers, Orthnell was in much better financial shape than many of the other Black men he knew in Middleburg. Perhaps it was in his nature, but he felt obligated to help his "brothers". So, he rented a small house in Titusville where he and four other men, Hokey Flowers, Bobby Stewart, Henry Lee, and Eddie Burkes lived. Orthnell, who by now was commonly referred to as Fredo, even by Lena, paid the rent, and never asked the other men for payment. "Fredo" is short for Alfredo, his middle name.

The work in the soap factory was anything but pleasant. The long hours and smells of boiling, processing hog and cow parts that were used to make the soap sickened Fredo. He was being paid $2.10 an hour, an amount he considered too small for the work he was doing. Even though he was only unloading and handling barrels of discarded animal parts, the whole environment was putrid with the odors of the parts being processed into soap. He ended up staying on this job only for a couple of months, until he landed a job at a restaurant, much more familiar territory.

In Titusville one of the nicest Motels was the Quality Court. Within the motel was a restaurant where Fredo would first wait tables, and then he was asked to fill in as a cook, which he was pleased to do. It seemed that somehow, going as far back as the monastery in the Bahamas that Fredo ended up in a kitchen. The men that Fredo brought with him from Middleburg also found work. Most of them ended up like him, in restaurants, working in various capacities. One of them, Horace, began working in construction and eventually would become a contractor with his own company. It is safe to say that Orthnell, by bringing Horace to Titusville helped set hm on the path to his life's work.

Over time some of the men moved back to Middleburg or elsewhere. As the men moved, more space freed up for Lena and little Orthnell to move in. It is interesting that Fredo saw helping the young men from Middleburg

Orthnell and Lena on their wedding day.

as important, if not more important than being with his family everyday, but that was Fredo's way. It didn't take very long, about 6 months, before the young men that Fredo was helping either found work in Titusville, like Horace, or moved on and Lena and little Orthnell could be permanently reunited with the man of their lives. By now it was early 1964, and they were together as a family. Mr. Towers took over the payments on Lena and Fredo's house and eventually sold it.

Fredo continued to cook at the Quality Court and Lena kept house. She also became pregnant that year with their second child. This time it would be a daughter, Marilyn Anne. Fredo was enjoying working at the Quality Court. He alternated between cooking and waiting tables, which he didn't mind doing. Fredo would be the only Black person waiting tables there, and as far as he knew no others had ever done so. Once again, Fredo was breaking into environments where others may not have been able to. Was it his charisma…His personality…His good looks? Today he believes that his accent was a key factor in giving people a level of comfort with and fondness for him. Waiting tables afforded him the ability to meet local people and even some celebrities like astronauts John Glenn and Neil Armstrong. They would often come to the Quality Court for lunch as the Kennedy Space Center was only a few miles away. Fredo also met Douglass Edwards, the famous CBS news anchor from about 1948 to 1980. Its proximity to the space center meant that the Quality Court and the economy around Titusville thrived. There were plenty of jobs and opportunities for ambitious men like Fredo. Everyone, it seemed, was happy.

As he worked at the Quality Court he formed and managed a band. He was approached about the band at a local hangout called the Duck Foot. The owner of the Duck Foot, Fred Harvey or "Uncle Duck" as he was affectionately called, after getting to know Fredo, thought he would be good for the task of managing a band. Fredo was not a musician himself, but had an ear for good music that was refined in Harlem, and before that, in the Islands. He was accustomed to hearing fine musicians playing a variety of instruments, and singers of traditional music, calypso styles, etc. So, it wasn't a completely absurd idea to Fredo and before long he had organized some local musicians who also hung out at the Duck Foot, calling themselves the Sandblasters.

ON THE ROAD WITH THE SANDBLASTERS

The Sandblasters included several musicians: William "Monk" Finkley played lead guitar, David Hall was on drums, Frankie Platt played the trumpet, Lonnie Stafford played the saxophone and Phillip White was the lead singer. There were two other musicians whose last names Fredo never knew: Frank played bass guitar and Leslie was on the keyboard. He also had three men who impersonated as female dancers and exhibitionists who over time became the band's main attraction. The only impersonator whose last name Fredo knew was Roosevelt Williams. The other two were simply called Scoffield and Lavern. Lavern apparently was a "knockout" when done up properly. This group of musicians and performers, along with Fredo as manager made for some interesting experiences and stories as they travelled and performed throughout Florida in some areas that were predominantly Black where they weren't very well known and White areas where they weren't always welcomed with open arms. They would travel by car and Fredo, being the manager usually drove the car that bore the trailer containing all of the equipment.

On one long, interesting weekend in early 1964, the band went on tour. Their first stop was up the coast in Daytona Beach on a Thursday night. They actually returned to Titusville after the show before getting up and heading to Hawthorne for a show on Friday night. Hawthorne is about 130 miles from Titusville, and having 2 more performances scheduled that weekend, they were planning to stay overnight in one of the towns where they performed.

COME ONE AND DANCE TO THE FABULOUS SOUL MUSIC BY **FREDO** AND HIS SOUL BAND, APPEARING NIGHTLY IN THE FAMOUS WOLF'S DEN, LOCATED AT THE RAMADA INN. SOMETHING DIFFERENT ALONG THE PLATINUM STRIP.

Fredo is the man at the front of the bandstand holding the cigarette.

It was in Hawthorne where things got interesting for the Sandblasters. There, the club did not have a bandstand or a stage. Performances took place directly on the floor with the crowd surrounding. Fredo warned the crowd to stand back and whatever they did, don't touch the dancers. Again, Roosevelt, Scoffield, and Lavern were very convincing impersonators. They were also the main attraction and on this night Lavern was dancing with fire sticks and doing a trick where he put accelerant in his mouth to blow fire. Well, as the crowd was gathered around and the show was going on, a man from the crowd reached over and touched Lavern's posterior, setting off a wild string of events. Lavern turned to the man and released a mouth full of accelerant on his fire stick as he turned and faced the frisky man. His hat and head immediately caught fire, evoking hysterical screams from the man and a complete halt to the performance. As the crowd moved quickly to put out the flames on their friend, a man claiming to be the man's brother, pulled a handgun and pointed it at Fredo. "I'm going to kill you," he told him. Fredo immediately pointed at Uncle Duck who was travelling with the band on this trip and told the man that he was the manager. The man walked over to Uncle Duck, pointed the gun at him and said the following: "Spell your name and if you miss one letter I'm going to blow your head off." All of the men understood the gravity of this situation and Uncle Duck, doing as the man said, also reached in his pocket to pull out about $80.00 to help cover the burned man's medical bills. This was enough to satisfy the one wielding the gun.

As things settled down the band quickly gathered their things and headed out nervously. As with other places where the Sandblasters would perform, the club in Hawthorne was small, all Black, and somewhat secluded. These factors all lent to the potential for serious problems if things went wrong as in this case. This being the mid-60s it wouldn't be prudent to make hasty calls to the police who were usually all White. They were playing in places where they were not known. And, being secluded meant that in the case of the man with the gun, someone, or all of them could have been shot and no one would have necessarily stepped forward to help them. This type of activity required the band, especially Fredo, who handled the bookings and payments, unless Uncle Duck was present, to be very savvy and alert, and he also began carrying a gun.

After they left Hawthorne, the band went on to play at some other locations that weekend staying overnight in a couple of other towns in central Florida. Roosevelt, Scoffield, and Lavern separated from the band and went north to Jacksonville before the mini tour was over and were arrested there at a performance for impersonating the famous Supremes. Fredo never heard from them or about them again.

Things were pretty quiet for the band after the incident in Hawthorne, until a couple months later. Fredo managed to get the band a gig at an all-White club in Titusville called the Green Leaf. The band was welcomed in just fine, set up as usual, and began to play. On this particular night Fredo was playing the keyboard, something he had pretty much taught himself to do while managing the band. Leslie, his usual keyboardist was not able to make it. They had played a few songs when a man came up to Fredo and whispered in his ear "the crowd doesn't like your music." As he looked around, he could see no one noticeably unhappy. People were drinking, socializing, and some were dancing. Fredo paid the man no mind and continued to play and he walked away. About ten minutes later the lights were shut off and the entire place went dark. Fredo and the others knew that this meant trouble. It was pitch-black and they were in unfamiliar territory. The men frantically began to try and gather their things and leave, but this was no easy proposition. As it became apparent that they would not be able to retrieve their things the band, Fredo included, tried to make their way to the doors. As they did, a man grabbed Fredo from behind with his forearm across his neck. "I've been waiting to get my hands on a nigger" he said as he squeezed and tried to take him to the ground. Fredo, resisting yelled "well, you got one!" as he opened his mouth wide and bore down on the man's arm with his teeth and all of his strength. He couldn't see all of the damage that he inflicted, but he could tell by the horrendous scream that he belted out that he broke skin at the very least. The man released him, and Fredo found his way to the doors, as did the other band members. By this time, Fredo had already pulled his firearm which he now carried with him at all times. Not being ignorant of his surroundings and the potential for "misunderstandings" in the minds of the police or anyone else, he did not wave his gun or overtly threaten anyone. He had it out discreetly to his side, just in case.

Once outside, the band was able to regroup and figure out their next move which essentially was to leave, and leave without their equipment which they could hear was being destroyed inside. Apparently, just as the man that grabbed him, some in the club that night simply wanted to wreak havoc, and it was no use for the men in the band to try and stop it for a number of obvious reasons. The better part of wisdom let them know that they should accept their losses and head home, which they did.

Life with the Band presented other interesting encounters for Fredo as well. While Lena, little Orthnell, and Marilyn were at home, Fredo worked and performed with the band and drew the attention of many young women in the area. It was hard for Fredo who was generally not prone to talk about work, his performances, or anything that he felt didn't pertain to Lena specifically, to keep from living a secret life in some ways. He was a young family man working to support them, but that was all that Lena knew. The interest garnered from young women was irresistible for him. In fact, on the night of the incident at the Green Leaf one of Fredo's girlfriends was there. Her name was Lois.

Lois was from Oakhill, FL, and met Fredo at a performance not long before the show at the Green Leaf. She was married, but her husband was in jail, so she was free to pursue Fredo, spend time with him, and travel to see him perform. Unless the band was travelling a long way from Titusville, Fredo would not stay anywhere overnight and made a point to make it home to sleep at least a couple of hours in his bed with Lena. Balancing his life outside the home and being a family man wasn't exactly easy though. At times, Fredo would have to exchange shirts with other men in the band if the one he was wearing had lipstick on it from Lois or another admirer. As far as Fredo knew Lena was unaware of his involvement with other women, but his choice of livelihood was taking a toll on his marriage and Lena began to express her discontent.

Not seeing her husband often and being left alone most days and also many nights with her 2 small children was not the life Lena envisioned for herself when she married Fredo, but that was what she got. She got Fredo the attractive bandleader. As she grew increasingly discontented with her situation and their relationship she urged Fredo to stay home more. She even asked him numerous times to quit the band, but he refused. Feeling as though it was his right and duty to provide for his family the way that he saw fit Lena's complaints and urgings often fell on deaf ears. Along with his right and duty to provide for his family the way that he saw fit Fredo was also attracted to the recognition and women that his life in the band afforded him. He kept this part of his life away from Lena as best he could, but it was nevertheless causing his marriage to unravel and moving he and Lena toward a separation and his children toward a broken home.

In 1969 things came to a head. Little Orthnell was 7 and Marilyn was 5, and Lena had had enough. She had been discontented for years and vowed to return to her mother Missy's in Middleburg. Fredo, not thinking she was completely serious or willing to leave him, still did not change. Lena waited 8 months to make good on her promise. One day, after finishing work at the Quality Court, Fredo came home to find his home stripped of everything except for his clothes and personal belongings. She had packed up all of the children's things and hers. She had even taken household items like the curtains that hung on the windows. What Fredo found that day when he came home was an empty shell that was once his loving home.

Fredo became furious! He grabbed his handgun, jumped in his car, a Chevy at the time, and sped away to Middleburg and Missy Mack's. It was his intention to shoot Lena for daring to leave him alone, especially with his children. As he drove though, something happened. He began to calm down and think about what he was planning to do and also the reasons why Lena left. After all, she had pleaded with him for years to stop working so much, leave the band, and come home to his family. By the time he reached Missy Mack's, 145 miles away, he had put his gun away in the glove box, and calmly approached the house. Upon entering, Orthnell and Marilyn immediately rushed to hug their father, and Lena stood back watching. It wasn't that there was no love between she and Fredo; in fact it was the opposite. She loved him so much she was unwilling to live in a marriage without having him consistently present and readily available. That day they were cordial and discussed their future. Once again Lena asked Fredo to leave the band. In fact, she wanted him to leave Titusville altogether and come and live in Middleburg, but again Fredo refused.

He stayed the night at Missy Mack's, played with his children, and in the morning Fredo returned to his life in Titusville. He and Lena agreed that he would come every other weekend to visit the children, but he made no promises about the future of their marriage. As time went on Lena and Fredo weren't able to rekindle and restore what they once had so they divorced. Fredo would move on. He would remarry, eventually leave Florida, and pursue things as he always had, just as he saw fit. Lena would never remarry and never leave Middleburg. In fact, she died there in 2012. She was a dedicated mother to the end and did all that she could to care for Orthnell and Marilyn.

Fredo continued to live in his and Lena's house in Titusville for several years. The divorce was finalized in 1973 and he continued to visit his children every other weekend and maintain a relationship with them, as best he could. This arrangement seemed to work pretty well for Marilyn, but for little Orthnell, he may have needed a little more consistent interaction with his father. As a teenager and into his adult life Orthnell Jr. was fairly consistently in trouble with the law. Lena, for some reason, didn't tell Fredo about all of the trouble that Orthnell was in, and Fredo eventually found out through some of his friends in Middleburg. He tried as any father would, to talk to his son and urge him to make better choices to no avail. Orthnell Jr. would continue his run-ins with the law well into his adult life. Marilyn on the other hand completed a degree in Business Administration at Bethune-Cookman University in Daytona Beach and has had a successful career in business since then.

Things for Orthnell Jr. may have been different had Lena allowed Fredo to keep his son as he wanted to after Lena left, but she refused. Fredo was devastated by being separated from his children and asked Lena to allow him to at least keep one. When that failed, Fredo had to settle for travelling to Middleburg on weekends and holidays to see his children. On one occasion, Fredo arranged to come and get Marilyn and take her to lunch. It was innocent enough in Lena's mind, but Fredo had other plans. They did go to lunch, just in Titusville! He "kidnapped" his daughter; at least that was how Lena viewed it. In his mind he had a right to his children and there was nothing wrong with having at least one of them come to live with him. Lena did not call the police or indicate any alarm, but she definitely wanted her daughter back.

Things were fine for a while with Marilyn staying with her father. Fredo lived alone, so there was plenty of room. Marilyn didn't complain and she was happy to be with her dad. Lena did not immediately come for Marilyn. In fact, just as she had done when she left Fredo with the children, she planned her actions very well. She found out that a woman across the street, Marion Thomas, her former neighbor was watching Marilyn while Fredo was at work every day. How she found out probably had to do with the fact that Marion was a distant cousin of hers, unbeknownst to Fredo. It's not clear how this bit of information eluded Fredo in the years that Lena and he lived in Titusville together, not far from Marion. One day when Fredo dropped Marilyn off at Marion's Lena came and got her. When Fredo arrived later that day to pick her up as he always did, he was furious to find out that she was gone. She was back with her mother. It was then that he discovered that Marion and Lena were related and that she allowed Lena to take his little girl. Fredo didn't immediately react and unlike Lena's first absconding, he didn't go for his gun or allow anger to overwhelm him. He simply accepted the reality that he would never have his children living in the same house with him again.

Not long after that, Fredo met a woman named Barbara, a nurse who had stopped by to eat at the Quality Court one night. They hit it off very well and would eventually enter into a long and serious relationship.

Lena, Marilyn, and Orthnell

PITTSBURGH

Fredo and Barbara had a happy life together. According to him they never legally married but were very close and loved each other. During this time Fredo left the Quality Court and began working at the Hilton in Cape Canaveral as a head chef. He was only there a month when something happened that would end his tenure. It was about 2:00 AM, close to the time when the kitchen was to close, and a man walked into the eating area. He wanted breakfast even though the kitchen was closing down. When the request for a meal of scrambled eggs, bacon, and toast came back to the kitchen, Fredo refused to prepare it stating "the kitchen is closed!" The waiter quickly asked him, "man, do you know who that is? That's the general manager." Fredo was refusing to prepare food for the person who was responsible for him being employed there and who could end his employment if he chose to. When he did respond it wasn't with something conciliatory or deferential. Fredo, in his typical confident way asked "does he know who I am?" and still refused to make the food. As the situation escalated, the manager walked to the kitchen and promptly told Fredo that he was fired. "No problem," Fredo responded and walked out, leaving his apron and chef's hat on the counter.

The next morning as Barbara prepared for work Fredo told her that he no longer worked at the Hilton and all about what happened. This was not a huge deal and Barbara was confident that he would find work again soon, which he did. His next job was at The Dutch Pantry near the Kennedy Space Center where ironically he would work the breakfast shift, again as a head chef. He stayed at The Dutch Pantry for about two and a half years. Fredo continued to work at restaurants and lounges throughout the 60s and 70s. He was even tapped to manage a couple of night clubs: The Red Top Inn in Memps and The Trumpet Lounge in Melbourne.

The way that Fredo arrived at the Trumpet Lounge was very interesting, not unlike many things in his life. In 1970 Lena filed a child support lawsuit against Fredo and he was arrested. While he sat in jail, a bail bondsman named Mr. Barber came around to see if men needed his services. He approached Fredo and asked him how much his bail was. It was set at around $250.00. Fredo agreed to utlize Mr. Barber's services and was released. The next day Fredo went to Mr. Barber's office to work out the arrangements for paying him back. They struck up a conversation that covered their life's experiences and what the situation was with Lena that landed him in jail. Through their discussion Mr. Barber realized that he knew of Fredo through friends of his. He knew that he managed a band and was well known in the entertainment circles around Titusville. Before parting, Mr. Barber asked Fredo if he had any interest in managing a lounge that he wanted to open in Melbourne, The Trumpet Lounge.

Once he was out, he went to Middleburg to speak with Lena and plead with her to drop the lawsuit and to let him know what monthly amount was agreeable to her. It wasn't that Fredo was neglectful of his children or didn't want to support them. It was just that he wasn't around them constantly and subsequently his monetary contributions to their upbringing weren't as consistent as Lena wanted. It may also have been Lena's goal to command Fredo's attention as she once did. Having him arrested was one way to do just that. They decided on $100.00 a month. Little Orthnell was now 8 and Marilyn was 6.

As manager of the Trumpet Lounge Fredo would be responsible for booking entertainment and handling payroll. His extensive experience with managing a band and working in restaurants and establishments that catered to people's food and entertainment tastes made him a good fit. Not to mention his personality, charisma, and good looks. It was a good fit for him, and met his financial and social needs until another opportunity presented itself.

While he was at the Trumpet Lounge Fredo met an older woman named Thelma Belle. He and Thelma developed an ongoing emotional and physical relationship. Fredo was never sure exactly how old Thelma was, but she had a daughter, "Retta", short for Loretta that was just slightly older than him. He was about 31 at the time. I will return to Loretta in a bit. Thelma was an enticement for Fredo in many ways. She was older, mature, had money and a house, and was enthralled in her young lover. When Fredo was on tour with the new band that he managed called Life, he would manage to stay nights with Thelma. She lived not far from the Trumpet Lounge in Melbourne, so it was a safe 50 miles from Titusville and Barbara and the two children he had with her in 1967 and 1968.

Barbara and Fredo had two daughters together, Parsonna and Robyn Renee. So, Fredo's family was expanding. He had four children now, two by Lena who was in Middleburg and two by Barbara in Titusville. It would not be long before Fredo would be on his way though, leaving behind Lena, Barbara, his four children, and moving to Pittsburgh.

It was Thelma's daughter "Retta" that helped open the door for Fredo's leaving Florida and the life he had there. Retta and her husband Bill Smoot had moved to Pittsburgh and were living in the Monroeville area, east of the city. They wanted to start a full-service restaurant in the then bustling East Hills Area and needed an executive chef. Retta reached out to her mother to see if she knew someone, and indeed she did. After speaking with Retta and Bill, Fredo began to seriously consider a move. Since his teenage years, Fredo's life had been adventurous and steeped in his desire to acquire a piece of the American pie. Perhaps this was another chance at doing that and as time wore on he leaned more in the direction of Pittsburgh than in the direction of his family in Florida. Barbara was not in support of the idea. She had two young daughters to consider, her own job and income, and she wanted nothing more than for she, Fredo, and their daughters, to continue their lives in Titusville. She also had ailing parents and she dreaded the thought of leaving them at such a critical time. With all this to consider Fredo did as he had done so many times before and relied on his internal belief in the need to chart his own course and not allow emotional and familial attachments to be a hindrance. He decided to pack up and leave, but believed that Barbara would eventually give in and come to Pittsburgh with the girls.

After letting Mr. Barber and his band members know, he packed up his Lincoln Mark III and made the roughly 1,000 mile drive to Pittsburgh. When he arrived in Pittsburgh, he stayed with the Smoots in their home in Monroeville on William Penn Highway. Bill had a job with the Housing and Urban Development department of the Federal Government and enjoyed a decent life in the suburbs. Bill and Retta assured Fredo that he was family and they made every effort to make him feel at home while the Restaurant was in the works. In fact the East Hills restaurant would stay in the works. Several of Retta and Bill's business partners backed out of the deal for some reason and the restaurant never came to fruition. It was disappointing for everyone, especially Fredo.

After the restaurant plans fell through Fredo continued to stay with the Smoots, hoping to land a job on his own. As he searched for work and bided his time, something unexpected happened. One day, after coming home from work and having a few drinks Bill and Retta began to argue. Bill became angry and got physical with Retta, inciting the ire of Fredo, who stepped in between the two. "What are you doing man?!" Fredo yelled at Bill, "Why you hittin her like that?!" "This has nothing to do with you nigga!" Bill responded. "Nigga!" Fredo said to himself. He had never heard Bill talk that way to him before, and it shocked him. After a brief moment of silence and stares between Bill and Fredo, Bill walked to another room and Fredo went to his room, not saying anything more to either Bill or Retta. Fredo knew that things would probably change in the relationship between him and the Smoots after that incident, but he didn't know how drastically and how soon.

The next day Fredo left out again to look for work, but when he returned that night he was surprised to find the doors locked and none of the keys that he had would open them. Bill had changed the locks. Fredo's time with the Smoots was over. He would have to sleep in his car that night and arrange to get all of his things the next day. Now Fredo found himself living in a new town and homeless. He took it in stride though, continuing to live out of his car, waiting for some sort of breakthrough. When he got the chance, he went over to the Smoots to get the rest of his things, going in the daytime while Bill was at work. Retta, feeling bad about everything that transpired worked to find Fredo a subsidized apartment, which she did. After two weeks of living out of his Mark III, he had a one-bedroom apartment at the corner of Bennett and Sterrett Streets in the Homewood neighborhood of Pittsburgh. This was the beginning of things turning around for Fredo after a pretty rocky start in Pittsburgh.

After getting the apartment, it wouldn't be long before Fredo would find work as well. One night at the Phase II night club, he overheard a young woman at the bar discussing with a friend how she had no one to take care of her two young sons while she went to school in the evenings from about 3:00 to 10:00. Fredo, thinking that this might be an opportunity to improve his situation, approached her, and offered to babysit her sons. Once again, Fredo caught a tremendous break. She accepted his offer. Her name was Alice Faye Isbell and her two sons were Damion, age 4 and Greg, age 6. He began watching the boys the following week and did so every weekday for about 6 months. Now with a steady income and an apartment, it seemed that his life in Pittsburgh might become permanent. This permanency was encouraged by the fact that Barbara doubled down on her resistance to moving to Pittsburgh, and the fact that Fredo and Alice began a romantic relationship.

Fredo and Alice began what would become the start of a lasting relationship, not because they would marry, but because they would have a child together. As they grew closer, and it became clear to everyone, including young Damion and Greg that Fredo was more than just their babysitter, he took on more of a fatherly role in their lives, something that would persist even as the boys grew older. Fredo and Alice would never permanently move in together, but their romantic involvement would continue pretty seriously and his role in Alice's boys' lives would take on new dimensions. A new child was added to the equation when Fredo and Alice's daughter Lottia was born in June of 1977.

Fredo now had 5 children. It became imperative for him to support them all and to get gainful employment. Again, he looked to the restaurant industry where he was comfortable. He landed an assistant chef position at an Italian Restaurant in Monroeville called Esta Esta. He began working there steadily and continued taking care of Lottia, Alice, and the boys. He would work at Esta Esta for a couple of years, then moved on to working as a head chef at the Interlude Steakhouse in downtown Pittsburgh and the Library, a night club that was owned by the same man who owned the Interlude.

Over the years, Fredo did his best to care for his children, visiting Florida when he could and sending money, and supporting Alice, even though their romantic involvement eventually faded. Fredo was a committed father and was a financial and physical presence in the lives of not only Lottia, but Damion and Greg as well, who to this day, call him "Dad".

One of the consistent themes in Fredo's life to this point was his connection to women, including his mother and grandmother, but also a strong desire to do what he thought he had to or wanted to do in his individual life. So, he worked diligently, pursued his career, but was never burdened with any regret or guilt about women who wanted more from him. In the case of his mother, she wanted him to stay in Andros, close to her. He left when he was 13. Lena, his wife, wanted him to quit the band and travelling and stay home with her and the kids. He refused, and subsequently lost her and had his relationship with his son and daughter permanently altered. Barbara wanted him to stay in Florida with her and their two daughters. He struck out for Pittsburgh. And now Alice wanted him to be the permanent father in her children's lives, something that could only happen if they married. They didn't.

Fredo was always singular in his mindset and didn't let emotional entanglements of any sort get him off course. He was pursuing the "American Dream" and anyone's story of success in America involves sacrifice of some kind. He had the passion, drive, and skills to make the dream come true, but he was a foreigner. He had left his base of support when he was a teenager and was fending for himself. There were people along the way to assist him, but much of his decision making and maneuvering was instinctual and not completely foolproof; those that he left in his wake, who loved him and wanted more from him, as he pursued his dream, were hurt. A mother yearns to be with her children, a woman marries with hopes of being with her lover forever, and children depend on and want to be with their father. Fredo reconciled these realities of disappointment and hurt with the reality that he did what he needed to do to "make it." It is true that had he listened to Rose, his mother, he may never have made it to the States; he may have been like all of his siblings and most of the people he knew back home and stayed in the Bahamas for good. Had he stayed with Lena and not pursued the life in the band he may not have developed the pedigree for management and entertainment and the connections that opened doors for him later. And, had he stayed in Florida, he may not have ever come to own his own restaurants and become the entrepreneur and culinary expert that he is known as today.

CHEF ALFREDO

People began calling Fredo "Chef" while working at Esta Esta and that name definitely stuck and became widely used when he opened his own restaurant in 1984. This was three years after he married Catherine Long, who he met while working at Esta Esta. The two were introduced by Chef's boss, and they hit it off right away. Catherine was pretty and very stylish. She enjoyed going out to dinner and clubs, and Chef obliged her gladly. They dated for about a year before Chef proposed. Catherine had a stable career; she was a sales representative for the Sears Roebuck store in Monroeville. This was important for Chef and played a role in helping to get him established in the restaurant business. With a stable home life and the support of his new wife he was able to strike out on his own. They bought a home in Penn Hills, another suburb of Pittsburgh and shortly after Chef had his sights on a location for his own restaurant.

The restaurant was located at 800 Woodstock Avenue in Swissvale. He named it Buckingham Catering. The name reflected his fondness for the English Royal Family. He didn't need to take out a loan for the business. The rent was low, only $275.00 a month, plus utilities. He used about $3,000.00 that he had in savings to buy the equipment that was there from the previous tenant, a woman who ran a pizza shop that she no longer was able to keep afloat. It was their intention for Catherine to help Chef at the Restaurant and maybe eventually leave her job with Sears, but that was not to be as she was diagnosed with Breast Cancer, not long after. It would be a battle that she fought for several years until she died in 1991. Before she died, Chef took her to treatments and was there for her however and whenever he could which was hard because of the restaurant. Eventually Catherine had to retire from her position at Sears and this led to the sale of their Penn Hills home. After the house sold, they began renting an apartment. Chef would even stay some nights at the restaurant in a small apartment that was attached in the back.

Not long before Catherine was stricken with Cancer, Rose, Chef's mother also was diagnosed with the disease. In fact, she came and stayed with Chef and Catherine for 6 months in 1982 while she underwent treatments at Magee Women's Hospital. Rose's treatments were successful and she returned to Andros. Little did he know that it would only be 2 or 3 years before his wife would be having the same struggle and he would be called on again to aid the woman that he loved in a battle for her life. After her recovery, Rose lived for a few more years, but a little more than a year after he buried his wife, he buried his mother in 1992. Joshua, his father had also passed away in 1991. So, 1991 through 1992 were trying years for Chef to say the least. He went home for both funerals and managed to stay for several weeks, leaving the restaurant shuddered while he was away. Before the 1990s concluded, he said goodbye to one more of his loved ones, his brother David, in 1994. He was only 42.

The 1980s were marked by illness for Chef's wife and mother, but it was also marked with an extramarital affair on behalf of Chef. Starting in 1980 he worked part-time as a bartender in Uniontown, PA at a place called the Disco Palace. It was there that Chef met Gail Petersen. They had an ongoing relationship that produced a son, Chef's sixth child, Alfredo Mario Russell. He was born in 1982 and Catherine never found out about the relationship.

In the 1990s, while he was in-between funerals, grieving, and travelling to the Bahamas, Chef was able to keep Buckingham going, developing a solid customer base, until 1996 when an opportunity to move to a bigger space, with a banquet hall presented itself. An influential local man by the name of Willie Beacham who Chef had come to know during his years in Homewood approached him about a building at 708 N. Dallas Street in Homewood and the potential to operate a restaurant. It was a club previously called the Zebra Lounge. Chef had been there once when it was in operation. "Mr. Willie" was thinking about buying it, but wanted Chef to operate the restaurant.

Chef went over and took a look at it with Mr. Willie, liked what he saw, and decided to end his lease on Woodstock Avenue. Buckingham Catering would have a new home.

The move to Homewood wouldn't happen right away. The place needed to be fixed up and made ready for the new restaurant. In the meantime, Chef would manage one of Mr. Willie's other establishments, Carl's Cork and Keg on the corner of Dallas and Kelly Streets, also in Homewood. Chef made enough money managing the bar to keep himself afloat, but he was anxious about getting his hands back in the restaurant business. This desire was exacerbated after one troubling night when the bar was visited by 5 federal agents. They came to shut the place down because Mr. Willie had never procured a liquor license. Chef knew that there was no license, but never considered the possibility of a raid. Plus, he was not the owner; Willie was. The five agents entered late one evening and cleared all of the customers out. Chef, being behind the bar and basically running the place, was the point man, the one the agents directed all questions to. One of the agents, the only Black gentleman, told him that he had spoken with Willie and let him know that they were going to shut him down. Willie being the man that he was told them to "do what they had to do," but there was no way he was going to voluntarily close his business. The only thing was that Willie wasn't the one there when the agents came; Chef was. They held Chef in the bar for a few hours while they measured the contents and the number of bottles in the place to determine the exact amount of illegal liquor that was there.

Eventually the agents finished their work and let Chef go home. They also found Willie a few days later and arrested him. This was the first red flag that Chef got concerning Willie's ways of doing business. He was hopeful that what had happened with the bar would not affect the restaurant deal. Before Willie was arrested, he and Chef had agreed for Chef to assume the payments on the restaurant, which he did not long after the bar was shut down and was just about ready. The payments were not actually paid to a bank, but to a person, Ms. Tonie, the daughter of the original owners of the Zebra Lounge. They had agreed to sell the place to Mr. Willie and Mr. Willie agreed to sell it to Chef. The problem with this arrangement was that nothing was in writing. Chef thought he could trust Mr. Willie, even after the raid on the bar, but that proved to be a bad choice.

Once Chef took over the payments on the building, he set up his restaurant calling it Buckingham Catering just as he had done in Swissvale. His business was successful in Homewood. He made many improvements to the building, adding a lounge/banquet hall in the basement, and making it a very viable place for entertainment and dining. In fact, it was there at 708 N. Dallas that I came to know Chef and got acquainted with his unique and tantalizing cuisine. Chef remained in this place for 10 years until something unpredictable occurred. Another associate of Mr. Willie, a man by the name of Perry began to claim rights to the restaurant and that Willie had agreed that he could have it. It is unclear what actually happened to Chef and Willie's arrangement other than the fact that Willie had, for whatever reason, gone back on his word. In hindsight, it was unwise for Chef to base his investment of time, energy, and significant funds on improvements and upkeep without a legal contract. He based everything on Mr. Willie's word. They did enter a small legal battle, but Chef was not willing to invest thousands more to hire a lawyer, so he cut his losses and left.

It wasn't so much of a loss though, as Chef had something else on the horizon. His exit from Homewood only provided him the reason to embrace his next opportunity. While he was still operating Buckingham Catering, he had been introduced to Nikki Heckman, who is now the well-known proprietor of Bistro to Go, a catering company and restaurant on East Ohio Street on Pittsburgh's North Side. In 2006, Nikki had decided to open a restaurant that offered a historic, bustling neighborhood quality, home-cooked food, hot, prepared and ready to carry out or eat in. A mutual friend told Nikki about Chef as a possible candidate for a Chef at Bistro to Go. So, Nikki went over to Buckingham and met Chef and tried his fare. She was impressed, and they agreed to meet to discuss the future. Chef knew that things with Buckingham Catering were untenable, and a partnership of some sort with Nikki seemed like a great opportunity, which he jumped on.

The only catch was that Chef did not want to simply be brought on to cook. He wanted a share of the business, which he got. Chef had already owned his own restaurants, had a large client base, and was well-known throughout the Pittsburgh area. These were all things that would help Bistro to Go thrive, which it has since October 2007 when they first opened the doors. Shares of the business were actually split three ways, between Nikki, Chef, and another partner, Joe Grondzlowski. Nikki and Chef primarily focused on the food, while Joe focused on managing the business.

As a new business, name recognition would be vital, and Chef was the man to make that happen. He began to go to various open-air food and farmers' markets throughout the city under the name of Bistro to Go, selling food and allowing people to sample what they could get plenty of on E. Ohio Street. The main areas where he did this were East Liberty, the Southside, Northside, and then outside of the city in Sewickley. This was a good way to advertise, but it also generated extra revenue for the restaurant and Chef. Initially, the proceeds went to the restaurant only. Chef didn't like this arrangement though. He, along with an assistant, for the bulk of the time, a young man named Tyree Lewis, were logging serious hours, and he felt that they should receive the bulk of the proceeds directly. Nikki and Joe, recognized the legitimacy of his position, and were obliged to do as he wanted. The restaurant was still getting the publicity, four days a week, every week, and the customers were beginning to come, and they all were happy.

Bistro to Go began to thrive and the 3-way partnership was working. Chef began to be identified with Bistro to Go and Bistro to Go with him. His client base from his previous restaurant locations was still supporting him and now the Northside was getting the benefit of feasting on his cuisine. Things would take a sudden and drastic change in the spring of 2009 though, never to be exactly like they were again.

Bistro To Go serves slow-cooked food fast

By MICHAEL MACHOSKY
Tribune-Review

Bistro To Go in North Side gives its customers the option of eating on the premises or taking their meal home.

SETH MURREN
TRIBUNE-REVIEW

In the best of all worlds, we'd sit down to nourishing home-cooked meals every night.

But in this world, even with a really good cook in the house (not me!), it's just too easy to stop somewhere on the way home or go around the corner for a slice of pizza.

So Bistro To Go's concept seems to have its niche already carved out — home-cooked meals that somebody else has been slaving over all day.

In other words, it's slow food, fast.

Sure, you're welcome to eat there. This sparkling new store-front along Deutschtown's securely main drag opens into a cozy, spacious room, splitting the difference between sleek urban bistro and Grandma's sunny, knickknack-strewn kitchen, complete with old-timey stove in the corner. But the emphasis clearly is on takeout.

Bistro To Go's kitchen roster is deep, with veteran chefs and cooks from the Ugly Duckling in Allegheny West and Alfredo's of Homewood.

A friend who was born in New Orleans says Chef Alfredo's Jambalaya ($10) is the real deal, and I'm inclined to agree. It's rich. It's hot. And it's just spicy enough to get your taste buds tingling — and made with enough tomatoes to make them jealous over at the Heinz plant.

Every day features new

lunch review

Bistro To Go

Hours: 11 a.m.-7 p.m. Mon.-Thurs., 11 a.m.-8 p.m. Fri.-Sat., 11 a.m.-4 p.m. Sun.
Address: 415 E. Ohio St., North Side
Phone: 412-231-0218

menu of sandwiches and salads.

The Thai Pasta Salad ($3-$8) is a cold wheat noodle salad with a strong complement of crunchy greens, cilantro, green onions, cabbage, honey-roasted peanuts and water chestnuts.

The Courtyard Chicken ($3.59-$6.50) sandwich is worth it for the fresh, soft baguette alone; the barbecued free-range chicken breast, aged cheddar and pico de gallo are just a nice bonus.

The Mr. Pepper ($3.50-$6.50) is named for its excellent thick peppered bacon, which is layered over mesquite-roasted turkey breast, provolone, lettuce and tomato, with just a touch of balsamic vinaigrette.

Bistro To Go also makes an effort to use eco-friendly containers and sells locally brewed pop from Natrona Bottling Co. I recommend the Mini Julep — kind of mild, many ginger ale — and the Pennsylvania Punch, which features actual grape flavor instead of purple-popsicle grape flavoring.

Here Chef is seen with the staff of Bistro to Go, including Joe (first on the left) and Nikki (second from the right).

Nikki, Chef, and Joe

THE ACCIDENT

On Sunday May 17, 2009 after service at Keystone Church in Hazelwood where he worshipped, Chef got in his van which he used for business and personal travel and headed for his apartment on the Northside. He left church and hit Rte. 376, the parkway. After travelling for a few miles, he reached the point where traffic merged from downtown and others veered off toward Pittsburgh's North Shore. Chef was driving in the far left lane, close to a jersey barrier when a man in a car, not paying attention to how far he was extending into Chef's lane caused chef to drive into the concrete barrier. He did not hit the barrier head on, but he still hit it in such a way that it crushed the front end of his van, totaling it, and doing significant damage to his legs and feet. His right leg was crushed and his foot was severed at the ankle. He was very disoriented after the accident and in desperate need of assistance, but he recalls looking down and seeing his foot in his shoe and unattached from his leg. He began to black out from shock. Fortunately, there was a Pennsylvania State trooper that wasn't that far behind the accident and was able to come to Chef's aid.

Chef recalls the trooper speaking to him, telling him that he needed help and that they would have to cut him out of the van. After that, everything went black. When he awoke again, he was in Mercy Hospital in downtown Pittsburgh where he would remain for close to one month, undergoing numerous surgeries to reattach his right foot and repair his legs and joints. After his care at Mercy Hospital, Chef was sent to a facility in the North Hills of Pittsburgh for rehabilitation, which included learning to walk again. Unfortunately, his right leg never healed properly, and after the onset of a very dangerous infection, it was decided that the best course of action was to amputate it at the knee.

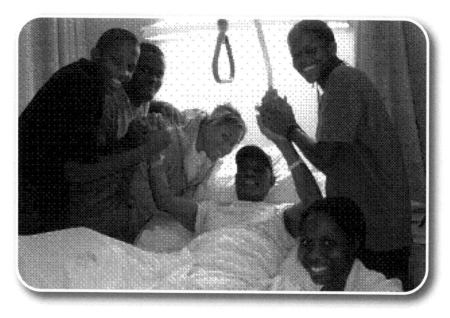

"Angels" as Chef called them – Students from the Bahamas studying in Pittsburgh who would come to visit and cheer. A friend, Herb Kolbe, who works at a local university would bring them periodically.

Though the amputation of his leg was devastating, it proved to be the best choice, as it led to the recovery of his overall health and ridding his body of infection. It would be a long time until Chef would walk again, something that many doubted would ever happen, but it did. In fact, he was eventually able to stand and cook again. While he was hospitalized, Nikki, his business partner, added an addition onto Bistro to Go called Bistro Soul, which would function as the strictly southern and soul food side of the business. It would be run by Chef when he was fully rehabilitated. Once he left the rehabilitation center, officially ending his hospitalization in October 2010, a total of over 17 months with his prosthetic leg and his newly learned faculties he eventually took over the operation of Bistro Soul until he was no longer able to do so as a full-time schedule proved to be a bit too much.

Chef at Bistro Soul.

IN HIS OWN WORDS (I)

Information About the Car Accident in 2009
I was on my way home from church when another car crossed into my lane and I crashed into a wall. There were four cars behind me when the accident occurred. I looked over onto the passenger side and I saw my foot sitting in my shoe. This meant that my foot was broken from my leg. That is all I remember because I blacked out.

I was dragged out and put in the ambulance and transported to Mercy Hospital. I stayed in the burn unit of Mercy Hospital and then was put in a private room. I stayed in Mercy Hospital from May 17 to June 12. I was then transferred to a rehabilitation center in the North Hills of Pittsburgh.

My daughter Marilyn assisted me in getting a room there. I was then transferred back and forth between Mercy Hospital and the facility.

My injuries were with my right and left legs. My right leg had more damage and also I had a staph infection which started during rehab. I had to go to the hospital for five days and then back.

One day I was waiting for the doctor. He examined me and informed me that if the right foot did not get better, there was no guarantee that I would walk again because of the damage that was sustained.

A couple of weeks later, Dr. Evans came to examine me. I told him that since I might not be able to walk again, would he amputate my leg. He stopped in his tracks and looked back at me and said that he wanted to make sure that he heard me right. When he said that, I repeated myself. Dr. Evans said he thought he heard right.

A month later, he came in and said that I would be transferred to Mercy Hospital to have the procedure performed. The next thing I knew, I went to surgery. After I went into the operating room for the surgery, I laid on the table and the next thing I remember I was in recovery with my limb in a stocking. This stocking prevented my limb from becoming swollen and infected. (I can recall Alfredo before and after this amputation. Before it his body had a very dark, sullen look, as if the infection was spreading and wreaking havoc on him internally. After it, he glowed as if the pall of disease was lifted. He was free!)

When I woke up, my daughter, Marilyn, and my pastor, Reverend Tim Smith, were there to greet me.

While in rehab, services performed by the nurses and aides were not always good. There was one instance where the aide did not properly clean me.

I had to go to therapy five days a week. This included learning to climb steps. There was an instance where my therapist hurt me so bad that I asked him if he didn't like me. He said, "You want to get better don't you?" From then on I never complained again.

Little by little, with the therapy, I became better and better. After a couple of weeks, the therapist took me outside and let me walk on the grass. This was to check my balance. The first time, I was pretty shaky. This was done three times to check my walking. Then the last time he said my balance was good. From that point on I began to improve.

I received three meals a day. Starting out I did not like the food very well, but I came to realize I was there for the long haul and I got used to the food.

While in rehab I learned how to drive in a wheelchair. I was able to meet some of the residents and make friends who encouraged me. One lady I met was Jerri Ransom and another lady by the name of Ginger. Other residents named Art Davis and Jim were all encouragers. They told me I would be fine. David was on dialysis and Jim had heart trouble.

Through all of it, I encouraged myself. I always said that with the help of God I would be healed. It took months and months for this to happen. I never gave up. I had the faith that I would be healed. I had no doubts. (I can attest to this fact. Many times I would go and see Alfredo and at times felt so sad for his condition that I shed tears, but not him. There was a tenacious faith present in him that I had never encountered before. I came to be the encourager, but ended up being encouraged.)

I left the rehab facility on October 24, 2010. I went to work, starting out working four days a week and up to seven hours a day. I drove my wheelchair backwards and forwards to work. After this, the Lord blessed me with a vehicle which was hand operated.

It was difficult for me starting all over again after losing my limb. I thank those who came to motivate and encourage me. They were Pastor Robert and Estelle Fulton, Pastor Tim Smith and his family, Opal Jackson, William Bishop and his family, and many others. One Sunday while I was in Manor Care, Pastor Timothy Smith came to my room and said that somebody wanted to see me. The surprise was that he brought the whole congregation from the Church which included Justin Smith, Priscilla, Jerry, Bunny, David Jones, William Bishop, and many others.

HOW GOD SHINES THROUGH

Fatherhood was a thing not displayed in his boyhood home. Joshua, his father, had seen no need to be involved in his life as a youngster. He only became so when Orthnell sought him out at the age of 13. It is safe to assume that if he had not gone to Nassau and found his father, Joshua may have been content to never see the son he had in Andros. Even though there were many nuclear families with stable fathers and husbands in the community where he lived and in his extended family, he had no male figure permanently in the home where he lived. Like his own, none of his siblings' fathers lived with Rose and her children. There are volumes today written on the impact of the lack of a father figure in the lives of children, but it is almost impossible to state definitively what the impact truly is on an individual as humans are all unique and the ways that certain things impact one will not necessarily be the ways that those very same things impact another. So, with that in mind and against the backdrop of Alfredo's upbringing, I felt it was necessary to explore more in-depth Chef Alfredo's decisions and actions as a father and how those choices have impacted his children. Most of the commentary that follows came from one-on-one interviews with three of his daughters: Marilyn Russell, his oldest daughter who he had with his first wife Lena, Robyn Russell, one of two daughters he had with Barbara Ingram, and Lottia Windham, his youngest daughter whose mother Alice Chef met when he moved to Pittsburgh. His fourth daughter, Parsonna has not been in communication with any of her family for many years, so I couldn't speak with her. I also was not able to contact his two sons, Orthnell and Alfredo, his youngest child, but their sisters shared with me as honestly as they were able to about their brothers' relationships with their father.

This, in my view, is the most important chapter in this book. Chef Alfredo's story is a remarkable one from start to finish, but his legacy includes not just his individual exploits regarding his immigration, work, and businesses. It also includes the lives of the women that he was involved with and the children that exist because of him and whose lives were shaped by him. These are the people who will carry on once his great life is over and that have had children of their own and are making their own marks on the world. Who he was as a father and how he related to them and their mothers has everything to do with what those marks look like and whether or not they have been able to thrive or not.

Chef Alfredo is one of the strongest, most resourceful and resilient people I have ever met, but the question is whether he was able to transfer his personal attributes of strength, fortitude, and resourcefulness to his children, most of whom he did not live with for the majority of their young lives. They had the experience, as he did, of not living in a home with their father, but unlike Joshua Russell, Alfredo has been present in other ways in his children's lives and has been a supportive father in the best ways that he can. This support and presence is reflected in the conversations that I had with his three daughters.

Of all the characteristics and qualities that Alfredo was able to share and impress upon his children, faith is the one that comes through in my conversations with all three of his daughters that I interviewed. All of them, without provocation or leading expressed genuine and passionate belief in the Lord Jesus Christ, something that they share with their father. Alfredo is not and was not a perfect man and intermingled with his triumphs were some failings, but one thing prevailed in his life and conscience from the time he left Andros as a young teenager. That thing is unwavering, unabashed faith. He couldn't articulate it then; he only referred to it as "the Spirit of God" that whispered to him directives and guidance as he stowed away and disembarked in a strange land, with little money, resources, and knowledge. All he had was an unidentifiable thing that urged him to push forward and not give up. This same drive and guiding spirit is present in his three daughters and this came through in my interviews. All of them are and have been for years involved in churches and one of them attended divinity school and is an ordained minister. Their walks of faith are not formalities or simply religious; they are real and have produced evidence of true faith and belief in the reality of God, not just a tacit acknowledgement of His existence.

To be fair, it was not just Alfredo alone that impressed upon his children the belief in God and the importance of faith. For example, Alfredo's first wife Lena was a very devout woman. In fact, her devotion to God is a part of the reason that she never could embrace Alfredo's affinity for night life and life on the road with his bands. She was a consummate mother. She married young and was completely devoted to her children and her husband. For her, life on the road or in nightclubs, even if it was supporting her husband didn't fit into the image that she had of motherhood, something profoundly impacted by her devotion to Christian ideals. She wanted to remain married and after she and Alfredo divorced, she never embraced the idea of a permanent separation with the young man that she agreed to live the rest of her life with and thus never remarried.

And so, it is a fact that Alfredo's legacy includes at least 3 of his children coming to saving faith is Jesus Christ and living their lives in a way that exhibits that faith and Christ's lordship. No one is perfect, but we all at some point should try to figure out why we are alive and what we believe, if life is to have true meaning. Alfredo is unashamedly given to believe God for the impossible, whether it be taking him over hundreds of miles of ocean or restoring him to health and walking after a tragic accident that took his leg but not the spirit that had been with him all of his life. That same spirit is in his daughters and their stories of faith are below.

Marilyn Russell
Now Lives in: Baltimore, MD
Mother: Lena Mack
Children: 3 girls (Paisley; Jordan; Chandler) and 1 boy (Kennedy)

Marilyn is Alfredo's oldest daughter and the one that he tried to "kidnap" and bring back to Titusville from Middleburg when he and Lena separated. She is Alfredo's second child; her older brother, Orthnell, is Alfredo's first born. Marilyn was very young, about 5, when Alfredo and Lena split up, but she was never very far from her father. She and Orthnell would spend weeks in the summer with him and he called often. She does not recall frequent visits throughout the year, but has vivid memories of extended stays with Alfredo and his second wife Barbara in the summer. Ironically the house that she would visit where Alfredo and Barbara lived is the same house that he and Lena lived in when Marilyn and Orthnell were very small.

Alfredo made no qualms about having the children of his first marriage spend time and get to know the children he had with Barbara, two daughters, Robyn and Parsonna, and Marilyn recalls that Barbara was very nice and loving towards her and her brother. A close relationship developed between all of Alfredo's children at the time and he saw to it that they would all feel like they were a part of his family. The only difference was that two of his children would eventually be leaving to go home with their mother and the other two would remain with Alfredo and Barbara. Marilyn recalls that she often wondered why Robyn and Parsonna got to live with Alfredo and not her and Orthnell, a question that any child would ask. As it was, Alfredo was doing what he could to both spend time with all of his children and make them feel a part of a complete family. Marilyn does not recall having feelings of resentment towards her father, just sadness that at the end of her stay she would have to say goodbye to him, and go home.

Young Orthnell undoubtedly wondered the same thing that Marilyn did: why couldn't daddy live with them, but he didn't express his disappointment as Marilyn often did. This may have been in part due to the number of male role models that Orthnell had in his life growing up. Several of Lena's brothers were involved in Orthnell and Marilyn's life, but especially Orthnell, because of sports. He was very athletic and a star from a young age in football and baseball, so he also had coaches that were heavily involved in his life and sports occupied a great deal of his time. So, when it came to lamenting or worrying about his father not always being physically present, Marilyn believes that perhaps these other outlets made that reality easier to cope with for her brother. Marilyn had her distractions as well; she was a very good softball player, runner, and was a high achieving student. In fact she graduated with honors from Orange Park Senior High School in Orange Park, Florida a year early, at 16. After graduation she attended Florida A & M on an academic scholarship. She graduated in 1985 with a degree in broadcast journalism.

As for Orthnell, he didn't graduate high school. Despite growing up in the same circumstances as his sister, being raised by Lena, having a host of relatives and coaches pouring into his life, and having a relationship with his father through phone conversations and visits in the summer, he wasn't able to complete high school and go on to what probably would have been a college career that included sports. Two of the relatives that were very involved in Orthnell and Marilyn's lives were Lena's brother Horace Mack and his wife Yvonne, the same couple that hosted Alfredo and Lena for their honeymoon. They stayed with Uncle Horace and Aunt Yvonne for stents in the summers as they did with their dad and Barbara. It was during the summer stays with Horace and Yvonne that Marilyn would take classes at their local high school to advance herself so that she could graduate early. Orthnell participated in summer sports leagues and camps in Port Orange, FL and Spruce Creek where Horace and Yvonne lived as well. Alfredo tried as best he could to be at games to support his son, and Marilyn recounts numerous calls to find out the results of games and to inquire how his son had performed. Alfredo also provided Lena with the money to send Orthnell to camps in the summer for his respective sports. Alfredo was not physically living with Lena and their 2 children, but he was present in their lives. He was not an absent father.

Today, Marilyn is closer to her father than Orthnell, but both still spend time speaking on the phone with him. Orthnell has commented to his sister that he enjoys talking with his dad and when they do speak it's usually for hours. Orthnell has spent most of his life in Middleburg, so he and his father do a great deal of reminiscing about the people and places where Alfredo once lived, had a career as a chef and a popular band leader, and knew many people. Marilyn mentioned how her and her father became much closer when he had his accident and was hospitalized. She visited him several times as he lay incapacitated in Pittsburgh hospitals. During these visits she had the long conversations and intimate moments that she missed as a child and younger adult. She learned a great deal about his faith, passion, and resilience. These things left a lasting impression on her and she speaks about them passionately when she discusses her father.

As with the other daughters that I interviewed, Lottia and Robyn, Marilyn is an active church goer. From her mother and father, she learned to embrace the Christian faith. This was evinced in the last stages of Lena's life. A series of health crises left Lena incapacitated and on life support in March of 2011. It was the doctor's recommendation to remove her from the support and allow her to drift off into eternity. This was against what Marilyn believed; so she

Orthnell in his baseball uniform

called her father who told her "miracles come in a crisis." This, along with a message at church that told her that whatever was going on with her, she was to "just stand" which meant don't give up no matter what, and it was just the encouragement she needed to believe God for the miracle. Well, after several days on life support, the miracle happened as her mother's vitals and organ functions rebounded enough to remove her from life support! Upon waking up, Marilyn asked her mother "do you want me to call Daddy?" Lena told her as she lay in the bed, "Sure, you can call Alfredo." When Marilyn got her father on the phone, she handed the receiver to Lena. "Hello," she said to Alfredo who immediately yelled, "Oh, my Lord!" He was ecstatic. The jubilance everyone felt was palpable. They believed God to do what the doctors said was impossible, and the Lord did it! Marilyn's referring to Alfredo as "Daddy" shows the affection she had for her father and the familiar use of that term around Lena. Lena's willingness and desire to reach out to Alfredo in such a critical time in her life shows her undying connection to him as well. It seems less like a family unit that was split apart for over 40 years and more like one that was as united and close as a family could be. It struck me as very interesting in speaking extensively with Marilyn that Lena never changed her surname back to Mack. Instead, she continued to use her married name, Alfredo's name: Russell. She never lost hope in what her and Alfredo once had, the love that they shared, and the family that they had begun together. And, here she was, many years later, very near death's door, and speaking to the man that she had never stopped loving.

Lena lived for almost a full year after being taken off life support. She remained in a skilled nursing home and died in January of 2012. Alfredo attended her funeral and spent a great deal of time with Marilyn and Orthnell and with other relatives and people he once was very close with on Lena's side of the family. Many years had passed, but just like Lena never lost her love for Alfredo, others hadn't either. He was still remembered as a larger than life man, a musician, a charismatic figure. Lena's family saw their splitting up in the early 70s as more of a mutual occurrence. The same is not true for Barbara's family, something that will be discussed in the next section.

Robyn Renee Russell
Now Lives in: Florida
Mother: Barbara Ingram-Russell
Children: One daughter, Erica

Robyn Russell is the younger daughter Alfredo had with Barbara Ingram. Barbara was a nurse at a hospital near the Quality Court where Alfredo worked for several years. Not long after their first meeting in 1966, they began dating and eventually moved in together. A bit of ambiguity exists regarding their marital status. According to Alfredo he and Barbara were common-law spouses. Yet, according to Robyn, they were legally married, hence her mother's hyphenated name. Regardless of the legal status of their marriage, they existed as a married couple and raised a family together for a number of years before Alfredo left for Pittsburgh.

The two daughters that Alfredo and Barbara had were Robyn Renee and Parsonna. They maintained an intact home until Robyn was about 10 and Alfredo made his move to Pittsburgh. It was Alfredo's original plan for his wife and daughters to come to Pittsburgh after he got established, but Barbara, not wanting to leave her ailing parents did not want to go. So, she stayed behind where she could help care for her parents and raise their daughters. This reality angered members of Barbara's family, anger that would eventually spread to Alfredo's daughters. They were bombarded with negative comments from disgruntled relatives on their mother's side of the family, and even though anger and negativity were never expressed by Barbara herself, the girls eventually became very bitter towards their father. This became especially acute in their teenage years. It was during those years and into early adulthood that Robyn and Parsonna realized what they had missed out on, not having their charismatic, talented, fun father around during the vital years of their development. During years when they needed his guidance, protection, and comfort as they navigated the world of junior high and then high school, dating, friends, sports, he was not there, and they were angry!

For Robyn, the bitterness and anger continued into her mid-twenties, until one day she had a serious, open conversation with her father following a blow-up between them. On this particular day she said some things to her father in a disrespectful manner and he sternly redirected her. She was a grown woman, but she stepped over a line with her father that she realized was not appropriate. This began the unravelling of the complexity of feelings and thoughts she had toward him and how they developed during her young life. As with Marilyn and Orthnell, Alfredo had never abandoned Robyn and Parsonna. He always called them and came to visit when he could, making the drive to Florida from Pittsburgh. He attended their graduations and other special events, and constantly tried to affirm their place in his heart and life. Yet, in their minds he still wasn't where he was supposed to be: at home with them and their mother. Like Lena, Barbara never married after Alfredo left and she kept the hyphenated surname of Ingram-Russell until she died. She also never lost her love for Alfredo.

Though Barbara never lost her love for Alfredo, she did lose a desire to live with him as husband and wife again though. In fact, she had the opportunity to marry him "again" in 2000. Alfredo had come to Florida for Robyn's wedding and brought with him a ring for Barbara. It had been almost 25 years since he left, but now he wanted the opportunity to reunite with his second wife. It didn't work. Time and circumstances had taken their toll. Though she was flattered, she declined his offer and Alfredo would have to be content with simply marrying off his daughter. There would be only one wedding. He would remain a bachelor and perhaps in his own way deal with the thoughts of what could have been. What if he had stayed in Florida? What if he had stayed with Lena or Barbara? What if he were closer to his children all those years? Marrying Barbara would have brought stability to his life and reconnected him with a place and people that defined life for him for many years. But, it was not to be. Alfredo left Florida after Robyn's wedding and returned to Pittsburgh.

After their blow-up the relationship between Robyn and her Father began to heal. Today they speak at least 3 times a week and she visits him in Pittsburgh regularly. Parsonna, on the other hand, has had no contact with her father since 2002. In fact, she has had no contact with most of her relatives since then. It was then that she and Barbara who was living with her moved to Las Vegas at the behest of a church organization that Robyn and Alfredo believe is a cult. According to Robyn and Alfredo she and her mother became involved in a strict religious organization and according to them members were forbidden or encouraged not to associate with people that were not also members of that group. During this time,

Robyn and Chef. As a child she idolized her father and wanted to be just like him, shades and all.

Today, she still loves her dad.

Robyn noticed that it was becoming harder and harder for her to see her mother. The effects of being involved with the organization were beginning to affect Robyn's relationship with Barbara. This was especially true when Parsonna and Barbara moved to Las Vegas. In fact, for over two years prior to Barbara's death in 2005, Robyn was not able to see her mother, and when she died the only possession that Parsonna allowed Robyn to have of her mother's was a pink ribbon from her casket. All of her belongings were in the house that she and Parsonna shared together. Parsonna would not allow her sister to go in, nor would she give her anything that belonged to Barbara.

Parsonna is still a member of that organization as far as Robyn knows and still residing in Las Vegas. The last time that Robyn saw her sister was a few years after Barbara's funeral. She went to Las Vegas and stayed with one of her uncles, Barbara's brother. While there she and her uncle went to where Parsonna worked. She was an employee of the Las Vegas Government and Robyn and her uncle were intent on trying to see her again. She went to the receptionist's desk and asked for her. The receptionist called back to Parsonna's office. When she came forward, Robyn and her uncle were standing there. She walked forward without moving close enough to embrace them and told them that she would be right back to speak with them. They waited for about 10 minutes before Parsonna's boss came out and told them that "Parsonna Russell doesn't want to see you and has asked that you leave the building." That was the last time she saw her sister or heard her voice. It was May 2006. This was definitely a low point in Robyn's life and exacerbates the reality that her family life has been less than ideal.

Despite the challenges that Robyn has experienced, she seems to be Alfredo's child that is the most connected with his family in the Bahamas and in the States. After her high school graduation Alfredo paid for her to go to the Bahamas and stay for 6 months with his family there. While there, she spent time with her aunts, uncles, and cousins, something that none of her other siblings have done to any great extent. Her younger sister Lottia is the only other one of Alfredo's children that has gone to the Bahamas, and though she met a couple of her aunts and uncles, she was only there for a week or so on vacation. In fact, Robyn still goes to the Bahamas on a yearly basis and has organized visits for members of the extended Russell family to come to the U.S. to visit as well. She has encouraged certain of her siblings to join her in her continued efforts to establish relationships with their father's family and connect with their Bahamian roots, but none to this point have grabbed hold of her vision and mission.

The reluctance for one of her siblings at least, Alfredo's last child, Alfredo Mario Russell, is perhaps a result of him not feeling close to his father. Robyn shared that he actually refers to Alfredo at times as "your father," as in Robyn's father, not his. It appears that of Alfredo's children, Alfredo Mario is the only one that has a rigid and non-familial view of his father. This perhaps is a result of him being the last of his father's children, and never living at all with him like all of his siblings at some point in their lives.

In July of 2017 Alfredo Mario's mother, Gail Kemp, formerly Petersen, passed away. She had spent some time in the hospital and had requested that Alfredo come to visit her, which he did. He also was present from beginning to end at her funeral and burial at the request of her daughter, who is also named Robyn. Even though Alfredo Mario wasn't the one who called and notified his father about his mother's death, he and his father spent some time chatting at the funeral and burial. This is an example again of less than ideal family circumstances, but ones that can't and shouldn't be ignored. Something has occurred in the process of healing and mending any breaches between Alfredo and his daughters that has not quite happened between him and his sons, or at least his youngest son. As stated earlier, Alfredo and Orthnell speak on the phone often at length and Orthnell shares with his sister Marilyn that he enjoys speaking to and connecting with their father.

Along with her dedication to her family and roots, Robyn is also an example of the miraculous. As in the case of Marilyn, Robyn is a woman of faith and learned from an early age to believe in God and trust Him. The first example of the miraculous was when a visiting minister prophesied at her church, Soaring Eagles International Ministries in Cocoa Beach, Florida, that she would learn to play the keyboard, something she had never done before. Within 3 years, she was the lead keyboardist in her church! Through observing the keyboardists at the church, practicing, and getting instructions from her father over the phone, she learned to play the instrument and to read music. It seems that Robyn inherited something from Alfredo: the ability and wherewithal to do things that seem impossible. Though he was not always with her growing up, he had instilled in her a belief in God and herself, and a lack of fear that would inhibit someone from doing unbelievable things.

Another miraculous feat and testament to the triumphant Russell spirit and the Spirit of God in her is her complete lifestyle change where she went from 320 lbs. and not being able to walk more than 20 minutes without severe discomfort to 170 lbs. and being able to run half marathons! Robyn was profiled in several sources, including the October 2014 edition of *First for Women*. The miracle began in 2011 when she grew tired of her situation and decided to make a change. Through prayer and looking deep within, Robyn slowly transformed from someone who was the epitome of unhealthiness to someone who everyone can look up to for inspiration and hope for change.

She explains in *Robyn Heals Her Chronic Skin Condition by Losing 127 Pounds* that her drastic lifestyle change came through natural means. She did not opt for surgery or fad diets. She made simple, gradual changes like refusing to eat late at night, cutting out fried foods, buying a Fitbit, and committing to an exercise regimen. In her words:

> I exercise seven days a week. Five days I go hard-core at the gym with either a high-intensity Spinning or Zumba class, plus weight training. On my light days, I do at least 5 miles of power walking and often switch things up so I don't get bored with my fitness routine. Sometimes I'll go skating at the rink, do some water jogging, or ride my beach cruiser for about 8 miles. The key is to stay active and keep moving. I wear a Fitbit daily, which is a great motivator, and I average anywhere from 20,000 to 26,000 steps a day ("Robyn").

As a result of her lifestyle change, Robyn said goodbye to bouts of depression, a leaking heart valve, a skin disease called hidradenitis suppurativa which she suffered from since she was 15, and a 48-inch waist. These are all of the things that she left behind. What she gained was energy, a bright and hopeful outlook, encouraging and enlightened advice for people who are living unhealthily and battling obesity, and a shelf full of medals from all the races that she's run. To date she's run over 33 races (4 half marathons, 4 ten milers, and a number of 5Ks) Oh, she also gained a 32-inch waist!

Robyn, like Alfredo defied serious odds. She acknowledges God in her achievements just as her father does and she acknowledges the discipline, encouragement, and advice that he has given her over the course of her life as keys to her success. The world is fortunate to have stories like Robyn and her father to draw on when we doubt and are facing what seems impossible. Again, in her words:

> I am stronger, healthier, and smarter, all because I chose to change the way I eat and start moving my feet! I'm much happier and enjoying life — taking control of my health was the best decision I could have ever made. I've been healed from the diseases that haunted me for years. I have more energy. I've been able to inspire and motivate others with my journey, helping to educate them on how to live a healthier lifestyle. Many people look up to me as their mentor; I'm grateful to have made such a positive impact on so many lives ("Robyn").

Lottia Windham
Now lives in: Dallas, TX
Mother: Alice Isbell
Children: One son, Noah

Alfredo's daughter Lottia is the child that has spent the most time with her father. She lived right in Pittsburgh and spent countless hours working alongside him in his Swissvale restaurant. She learned many lessons from her father, but like his other children she didn't have the experience of her dad having a committed long-term marriage to her mother. Alfredo was a dedicated and loving father, but like most children would, she wanted her father to love her mother enough to marry her and stay married to her and "live happily ever after".

Actually, her mother Alice and Alfredo never married at all. It was something that Alice and all of her children wanted, but it was not to be. Lottia and her two brothers loved Alfredo and he was devoted to them. Lottia has fond memories of many hours spent with her father on fishing trips and family outings to state parks. Her brothers loved him as well, even though he was not their biological father. They called him "Dad" and still do. Even though Lottia has fond memories of trips to state parks to fish and picnic and numerous other activities, most of her quality time with her father came at Alfredo's Buckingham restaurant. As she describes it: "it was all hands on deck," when it came to her father's restaurant.

Lottia and her brothers worked at Buckingham for many hours on many days, especially in the summer months, when school was out. The boys being older, and also not Alfredo's natural sons, the expectation for them to work was not quite as strict as it was for Lottia. She was expected to work alongside her dad several days out of every summer week starting in elementary school. She recalls doing all sorts of things pertaining to her father's restaurant and even enjoying some of them. She shopped with him, replenished needed supplies, helped prepare foods, and accompanied him on catering jobs. Work at the restaurant and riding to restaurant supply stores and markets in Pittsburgh's Strip District provided Lottia with hours of undivided time with her father, time that served to shape various aspects of her own personality and character as Alfredo taught her valuable lessons about business and life.

One of the things that became permanently a part of her character was the value of hard work. During the summers when her friends were sleeping in and hanging out at the pools and relaxing, Lottia was getting up early and taking trips to get supplies for her father's restaurant, serving as his little prep cook, or assisting on a catering job. One of the things she remembers vividly and maybe was even traumatized by was peeling shrimp. She recalls having to peel countless pounds of the crustaceans. As an expert in Cajun dishes, shrimp was a staple of Alfredo's cuisine, and of course, the shrimp had to be peeled. So, every day that she went to work with her dad, he needed the help of her nimble little fingers in extracting the plump, tender shrimp from their thin, tough shell. And that is exactly what she did for hours at a time, so that her father could simply reach over into dozens of pounds of clean, ready to cook shrimp to work his magic on and keep his family fed. Lottia learned the value of hard work from these days with her father, but she also developed an aversion to shrimp! To this day, she will not eat them. It was a small price to pay for a part of her character that has led her to complete two degrees, become an ordained minister, and remain a constantly employed and productive mother, someone her teenage son, Noah, looks up to and admires.

Lottia earned a BA in education with a minor in psychology from the California University of Pennsylvania, but her passion after she finished school was for Christian ministry. After finishing at California University of Pennsylvania she attended Judah Training Institute in Washington, PA and gained an associate's degree in youth pastoring. When she completed her associate's degree she joined the staff at The Lord's Church in Monroeville, PA. While there she served as the youth pastor and organized one of the largest gatherings of Christian youth in the area for several years. It was called Summer Jam and was attended by hundreds of area youth, both Christian and non-Christian, over the years. In fact, as I worked with youth in the Church community in Pittsburgh I often heard about the annual youth event put on by The Lord's Church, but never had the opportunity to attend.

When she decided to move to Dallas, Lottia continued her dedicated work for God at Rock City Church. There she was the Director of Youth from 2004 to 2012. While in this role she facilitated a summer camp, and oversaw several other ministries as she continued to walk out the Lord's calling on her life. Nowadays she attends a new church called Covenant Church. She is not as active as she once was and spends more time attending to Noah who is involved in a number of activities as many teenagers are.

Lottia gained an appreciation for hard work and a sense of faith from Alfredo, but it wasn't until she was older when a very important conversation between her and her father helped her realize truly what he meant to her and how he would ultimately shape her life. For many years of her life she had admired her father, but she didn't always enjoy being around him. He was stern and blunt in his dealings with just about everyone, including her. To her, interactions with her dad felt more like business transactions than a loving father-daughter relationship. Then, something happened. When she was 18, she wanted to buy a car, but being young and having no credit history, she needed a co-signer. Naturally, she went to the most responsible, established person she knew: her father.

She went over to Buckingham where she knew her father would be and approached him with the idea. His response was "it's nice that you want a car, but that's not what you need right now." In her mind she thought, "I don't want a life lesson or a lecture! I want you to be a loving father who gives his daughter what she wants!" But that wasn't Chef and she knew it. Instead, he sat her down, right there where she had spent so many days, months, and years helping him, and they had a lengthy talk. He began to share with her his story, the very story that you have read in the pages of this book. She, for the first time learned the harrowing tales of how her father left the Bahamas as a young teen and stowed away, how he went to Florida and New York, how he was a chauffeur and butler for a wealthy White family, how he taught himself to play the piano and managed bands and night clubs, and all the other things that led to him owning the very business where they now sat.

It was at this moment when she truly appreciated who her father was and the sacrifices he had made to bring him to that point. Something about his story, the details that she had not fully known before, made the stern manner with which he dealt with her and most others, and the unforgiving sense of dedication to work and success that he displayed all her life, something to not loathe as she had often done, but something to admire and emulate. In fact, in our conversation, Lottia commented that the thing that looms the largest in her thoughts about her father and his impact on her is his work ethic. She has never had a sense of entitlement or embraced the idea that anyone owed her anything just for existing. Like her father, she believes in working and working hard. Eventually, when she was a little older, had finished college, and saved up some money, she bought her first car on her own.

Lottia and her dad at her "Sweet 16" celebration in a park in Pittsburgh.

Lottia, Noah, and Chef.

THE LATEST CHAPTER

Chef is now semi-retired. He is called upon to cook for special events at Bistro to Go, like the Mardi Gras feast and celebration held there every year in February. He is the focal point of the event as he serves up homemade jambalaya, Cajun shrimp and rice, gumbo, and his famous Chicken Isabell. He remains a household name and countless people in the Pittsburgh area associate him with the restaurant, even though he is not there every day. As this book explains he was vital in the establishment of the business and the building of its client base. His work of going to farmers' markets and open-air gatherings in his van to sell and serve his delicious cuisine under the banner of Bistro to Go undoubtedly led to it becoming as popular as it is today. This cannot be forgotten or ignored any more than the Buckingham Restaurant can be. There are still people throughout the Pittsburgh area that remember Chef Alfredo and his Cajun fare as he labored, served, and satisfied individuals and families for over 40 years.

In the process of writing this book, a young man who works with me in the school where I teach saw the unfinished manuscript for this book out on my desk one day and began to thumb through it. As he did, he experienced a remarkable revelation. As he looked at the title page with the image of Alfredo in his finest Chef's attire and read some of the pages he realized that it was Buckingham that his father often took him to when he was a child growing up in Swissvale. When he saw me he was ecstatic. As he described for me what it meant for him to read parts of my manuscript and to know that there was a book being written about Chef Alfredo, I realized that the impact and importance of his life was more than I knew. This gave me the confidence to continue with the project and see it to completion. I knew that God was in it and that it was meant to be. It had been over 10 years since I started and at times wondered if I would ever finish or if it would ever be published. When I told Chef about this encounter he was overjoyed and we celebrated the significance of it together. We both knew that we had to finish and that the world needed to know of his story.

Today Alfredo is 82 years old and planning his next restaurant venture, a pizza shop that features pizzas with a Cajun twist. He is as excited as he ever was about what God has in store for him. He first learned to cook as a young teenager at St. Augustine's monastery and over 60 years later he is still doing that which he believes God purposed him to do. To talk to Chef Alfredo now is to talk to a man who plans to end his life the way that he started it: fulfilling a dream, answering the call of the Spirit, and stretching the limits of his own humanity. It is remarkable indeed. There is no notion of "retirement" in Chef's way of thinking. He will work to the very end. As for now, he only thinks about living. He is looking for a location and lining up investors for his new restaurant and some land development in the Bahamas. Perhaps this book will aid in that endeavor. Orthnell Alfredo Russell is a true lesson in the life lived well. God has blessed him indeed. And, we are blessed for knowing his story.

Chef currently lives on Pittsburgh's North Side, less than three blocks from Bistro to Go. His home is the same apartment that he rented before the accident in 2009. It is now equipped for a person with an injury like his, something he had to fight for. He also drives a van that has been equipped with an accelerator and brake mechanism on the steering wheel. It took Chef over six months to learn how to drive it and had to pass a test to get a special license to legally be on the road. In every way he has shown the will to live and the will to live the way he wants. He isn't perfect, but he is a fighter and proves that we all can go beyond physical limitations to achieve whatever it is that we want to do. From stowing away at 15 to getting his apartment handicap accessible and learning to drive a modified vehicle without the use of his legs, he has had to harness the confidence and belief in himself to get what he knows he deserves.

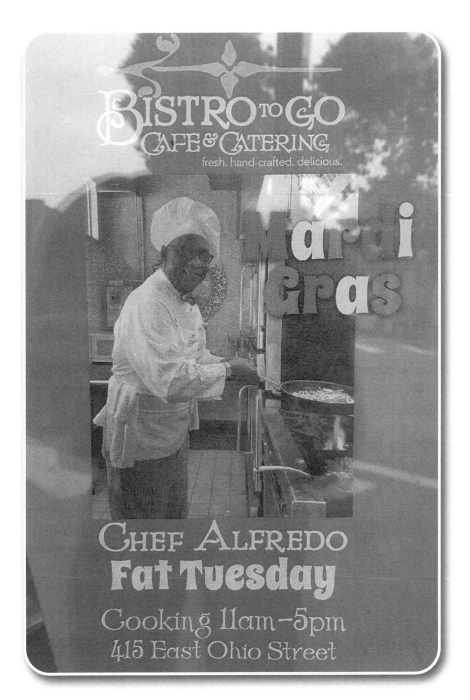

A flyer advertising Bistro to Go's annual Mardi Gras event

Chef in his modified van.

Whether he went by "Orthnell", "Alfredo", "Fredo", or "Chef" he has been an inspiration to many people that have known him. His story evokes feelings of accomplishment and achieving despite unfavorable odds. He started with no material wealth. What he had was a loving family, a strong community, unfailing faith in God, and resolve. With these he made his way to America. He didn't let his lack of legal status or resources dash his hopes or cause him to end his quest. He lives his life as he sees fit and is his own man. It doesn't mean that no one was hurt along the way, but it does show that men, at times, have to make tough decisions, right or wrong, and live with those decisions. It just may be that when you do that someone one day may write a book about you. It seems that he was born to cook. It takes much more than training though to be the best at anything. For him it also took personality, charisma, bravery, and at times sheer fate to get into the choice, favored positions that made him notable and are markers of true success. The Bahamas, Florida, New York, and Pittsburgh are all places that were graced by Chef's presence and were impacted by this remarkable man.

Hopefully the preceding pages inspire you to realize your dreams and find the wherewithal to achieve them at all costs. After all, this moment in this day is all that is guaranteed to any of us and it behooves us all to make the most of it.

SOME OF
Chef Alfredo's
SIGNATURE RECIPES

Alfredo's Island Shrimp Curry

3 Tablespoons of vegetable oil
3 Tablespoons of butter
2 Mild onions chopped fine
2 Tablespoons of garlic powder
1 lime
3 Lbs. of large raw shrimp
1 Green pepper chopped fine
1 Red pepper chopped fine
Salt to taste
A little hot pepper sauce
A little Chablis wine

Directions:
Heat the butter and oil in a large skillet. Sauté peppers and onion in the skillet. Add garlic powder and cook for 15 minutes on very low. Add shrimp and cook covered for 8 minutes on medium heat until shrimp are firm and pink. Don't overcook the shrimp! Add hot pepper sauce and Chablis wine to taste. Serves 4. Serve with rice or Cajun potatoes.

Alfredo's Simple Shrimp Creole

2 Tablespoons butter or margarine
½ Cup minced onion
2 Tablespoons flour
1 Bay leaf (crushed)
¼ Cup diced celery
1 Tablespoon minced parsley
½ Cup minced bell pepper
Dash of cayenne pepper
½ Teaspoon tabasco sauce
1 Tablespoon tomato paste
½ Teaspoon salt
3 Cup water
2 Cup Cooked shrimp
1 Cup cooked rice

Directions:
Melt butter in heavy skillet; sauté onion until translucent, but not browned. Combine flour, bay leaf, celery, parsley, bell pepper, cayenne pepper, tabasco sauce, tomato paste, and water. Simmer for 30 minutes over low heat, stirring occasionally until thickened. Stir in the shrimp and simmer for an additional 20 minutes. Serve over rice.

Alfredo's Famous Chicken Isabell

5 Ozs. chicken breast, deboned, and cut into small pieces
1 Teaspoon paprika
1 Cup mushrooms, sliced
¼ Teaspoon of white pepper
½ Cup Chablis wine
⅓ Cup butter
1 Onion, sliced
1 Bunch scallion tips, diced
1 Tomato, sliced
½ Teaspoon garlic powder

Dust chicken in flour and sauté with all ingredients, except tomato and Chablis. Sauté for 12 minutes or until tender. Stir in paprika for color, then add tomato and Chablis. Add salt to taste. Serve over rice or pasta. Serves 2 (goes well with wine).

Alfredo's Jamaican Patties

Filling:

2 Tablespoons vegetable oil or yellow cooking butter

1 Large onion, finely chopped

2 Cloves garlic, finely chopped

2 Fresh hot peppers, seeded and finely chopped

1 Sprig fresh thyme, finely chopped

4 Sprigs fresh chives, finely chopped

2 Sprigs fresh parsley, finely chopped

¾ Lb. prime ground beef, chicken, or fish

¼ Teaspoon fresh ground turmeric or annatto

¼ Teaspoon fresh ground ginger

¼ Teaspoon ground cumin

1 Teaspoon allspice

½ Teaspoon cardamom

1 Tablespoon Jamaican rum

Heat the oil or cooking butter in a frying pan and then add annatto seed. Cook for a minute or two, until the seeds have given up their color. Remove the seeds with a slotted spoon and discard. Add the beef and brown it. Break it up with a fork as it browns. Add the onion and garlic and cook until the onion is tender. Continue to cook and add the other ingredients.

Shell:

4 Cups plain flour

1 Tablespoon ground dried turmeric or annatto

1 Teaspoon salt

4 Tablespoon cold water

1 Cup butter (softened)

3 ounces (6 Tablespoons) lard

Sift the flour and salt into a bowl. Divide the butter and lard into 4 equal parts. Rub 1 part each of butter and lard into the flour with enough cold water to make elastic dough. Roll out the dough onto a floured board into a strip about 8 inches wide. Cut 1 part each of the remaining butter and lard into small pieces and dot ⅔ of the pastry with it. Dredge lightly with flour. Fold the section without the butter and lard over the middle one third of the pastry strip. Then fold the first portion over to form a square. Press the open edges lightly together with a rolling pin to prevent air from escaping and turn the pastry so that it faces you. Roll the pastry into a strip as before and repeat the process until the remaining butter and lard is used. Wrap the pastry in waxed paper and refrigerate for at least 1 and a ½ hours before using.

- The End -

WORKS CITED

Buchanan, Leigh. "The U.S. Has 27 Million Entrepreneurs." *Inc.com*. Inc.,
02 Sept. 2015. Web 23 May 2017.

"Eastern Acquired Mackey Air." *The EAL Radio Show & EAL Radio Latino*,
www.ealradioshow.com/eastern-acquired-mackey-air.

"The History of Eastern Air Lines 1929-1991." *Silverliners*, www.thesilver-
liners.org/library/thehistory-of-eastern-air-lines.cfm.

"Robyn Heals Her Chronic Skin Condition by Losing 127 Pounds." *Every-
dayHealth.com*, 27 August 2015,
www.everydayhealth.com/columns/weight-loss-success-stories/robyn-
heals-chronic-skin-condition-by-losing-pounds/.